BIG BOOK
OF MATH FOR
MINECRAFTERS

ILLUSTRATED BY AMANDA BRACK

Sky Pony Press
New York

Copyright © 2018 by Hollan Publishing, Inc.

Minecraft® is a registered trademark of Notch Development AB.

The Minecraft game is copyright © Mojang AB.

All rights reserved. No part of this book may be reproduced in any manner without the express written consent of the publisher, except in the case of brief excerpts in critical reviews or articles. All inquiries should be addressed to Sky Pony Press, 307 West 36th Street, 11th Floor, New York, NY 10018.

Sky Pony Press books may be purchased in bulk at special discounts for sales promotion, corporate gifts, fund-raising, or educational purposes. Special editions can also be created to specifications. For details, contact the Special Sales Department, Sky Pony Press, 307 West 36th Street, 11th Floor, New York, NY 10018 or info@skyhorsepublishing.com.

Sky Pony® is a registered trademark of Skyhorse Publishing, Inc.®, a Delaware corporation.

Minecraft® is a registered trademark of Notch Development AB.
The Minecraft game is copyright © Mojang AB.

Visit our website at www.skyponypress.com.

Authors, books, and more at SkyPonyPressBlog.com.

10 9 8 7 6 5 4 3 2

Library of Congress Cataloging-in-Publication Data is available on file.

Cover art by Bill Greenhead

Cover design by Brian Peterson

Interior art by Amanda Brack

Book design by Kevin Baier

Print ISBN: 978-1-5107-3759-4

Printed in China

CONTENTS

MATH FACTS FOR MINECRAFTERS

MATH FOR MINECRAFTERS

WORD PROBLEMS FOR MINECRAFTERS

MATH FACTS FOR
MINECRAFTERS
Addition & Subtraction

grades 1-2

A NOTE TO PARENTS

When you want to reinforce classroom skills at home, it's crucial to have kid-friendly learning materials. This *Math Facts for Minecrafters* workbook transforms math practice into an irresistible adventure complete with diamond swords, zombies, skeletons, and creepers. That means less arguing over math practice and more fun overall.

Math Facts for Minecrafters is also fully aligned with National Common Core Standards for 1st and 2nd Grade Math. What does that mean, exactly? All of the problems in this book correspond to what your child is expected to learn in school. This eliminates confusion and builds confidence for greater academic success!

As the workbook progresses, the math practice sheets become more advanced. Encourage your child to progress at his or her own pace. Learning is best when students are challenged but not frustrated. What's most important is that your Minecrafter is engaged in his or her own learning.

To measure progress and determine your child's overall fluency in solving math facts, you may want to use a timer. A child who is fluent will recall the answer to a math fact within 3 seconds. Once your child can accurately and consistently complete a full 20-problem page in 60 seconds, he or she is showing proficiency in that category of math facts.

Whether it's the joy of seeing their favorite game characters on every page or the thrill of seeing the progress they're making, this workbook is designed to entice even the most reluctant student.

Happy adventuring!

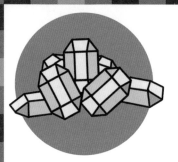

CONTENTS

MATH FACTS PROGRESS TRACKER

Date	Page Number or Skill Practiced	Number Correct in One Minute

ADDITION MATH FACTS WITH 0 AND 1

1. $\begin{array}{r} 7 \\ +\,0 \\ \hline \end{array}$ 2. $\begin{array}{r} 5 \\ +\,1 \\ \hline \end{array}$ 3. $\begin{array}{r} 2 \\ +\,1 \\ \hline \end{array}$ 4. $\begin{array}{r} 9 \\ +\,1 \\ \hline \end{array}$ 5. $\begin{array}{r} 7 \\ +\,1 \\ \hline \end{array}$

6. $\begin{array}{r} 6 \\ +\,0 \\ \hline \end{array}$ 7. $\begin{array}{r} 3 \\ +\,1 \\ \hline \end{array}$ 8. $\begin{array}{r} 0 \\ +\,3 \\ \hline \end{array}$ 9. $\begin{array}{r} 4 \\ +\,0 \\ \hline \end{array}$ 10. $\begin{array}{r} 10 \\ +\,0 \\ \hline \end{array}$

11. $\begin{array}{r} 8 \\ +\,0 \\ \hline \end{array}$ 12. $\begin{array}{r} 0 \\ +\,0 \\ \hline \end{array}$ 13. $\begin{array}{r} 2 \\ +\,0 \\ \hline \end{array}$ 14. $\begin{array}{r} 6 \\ +\,1 \\ \hline \end{array}$ 15. $\begin{array}{r} 8 \\ +\,1 \\ \hline \end{array}$

16. $\begin{array}{r} 9 \\ +\,0 \\ \hline \end{array}$ 17. $\begin{array}{r} 1 \\ +\,0 \\ \hline \end{array}$ 18. $\begin{array}{r} 3 \\ +\,0 \\ \hline \end{array}$ 19. $\begin{array}{r} 5 \\ +\,0 \\ \hline \end{array}$ 20. $\begin{array}{r} 4 \\ +\,1 \\ \hline \end{array}$

ADDITION MATH FACTS WITH 0 AND 1

1. 8
   + 0
   ___

2. 5
   + 1
   ___

3. 2
   + 0
   ___

4. 9
   + 1
   ___

5. 6
   + 1
   ___

6. 4
   + 0
   ___

7. 8
   + 1
   ___

8. 0
   + 3
   ___

9. 6
   + 0
   ___

10. 10
   + 0
   ___

11. 7
   + 0
   ___

12. 0
   + 0
   ___

13. 2
   + 1
   ___

14. 7
   + 1
   ___

15. 3
   + 1
   ___

16. 9
   + 0
   ___

17. 5
   + 0
   ___

18. 3
   + 0
   ___

19. 1
   + 0
   ___

20. 4
   + 1
   ___

SUBTRACTION MATH FACTS WITH 0 AND 1

1. 7
   − 0

2. 5
   − 1

3. 2
   − 1

4. 9
   − 1

5. 7
   − 1

6. 6
   − 0

7. 3
   − 1

8. 3
   − 0

9. 4
   − 0

10. 10
    − 1

11. 8
    − 0

12. 0
    − 0

13. 4
    − 0

14. 6
    − 1

15. 8
    − 1

16. 9
    − 0

17. 1
    − 0

18. 2
    − 0

19. 5
    − 0

20. 4
    − 1

SUBTRACTION MATH FACTS WITH 0 AND 1

1. 8
    − 0

2. 0
    − 0

3. 9
    − 1

4. 6
    − 1

5. 8
    − 1

6. 7
    − 0

7. 1
    − 0

8. 1
    − 1

9. 5
    − 0

10. 4
     − 1

11. 6
     − 0

12. 5
     − 1

13. 3
     − 1

14. 10
     − 1

15. 7
     − 1

16. 9
     − 0

17. 4
     − 0

18. 3
     − 0

19. 2
     − 1

20. 2
     − 0

ADDITION MATH FACTS FROM 0 TO 10

1. $\begin{array}{r} 2 \\ + 4 \\ \hline \end{array}$

2. $\begin{array}{r} 3 \\ + 5 \\ \hline \end{array}$

3. $\begin{array}{r} 2 \\ + 8 \\ \hline \end{array}$

4. $\begin{array}{r} 7 \\ + 2 \\ \hline \end{array}$

5. $\begin{array}{r} 6 \\ + 3 \\ \hline \end{array}$

6. $\begin{array}{r} 4 \\ + 4 \\ \hline \end{array}$

7. $\begin{array}{r} 8 \\ + 1 \\ \hline \end{array}$

8. $\begin{array}{r} 3 \\ + 3 \\ \hline \end{array}$

9. $\begin{array}{r} 2 \\ + 5 \\ \hline \end{array}$

10. $\begin{array}{r} 2 \\ + 3 \\ \hline \end{array}$

11. $\begin{array}{r} 5 \\ + 5 \\ \hline \end{array}$

12. $\begin{array}{r} 3 \\ + 7 \\ \hline \end{array}$

13. $\begin{array}{r} 4 \\ + 5 \\ \hline \end{array}$

14. $\begin{array}{r} 5 \\ + 3 \\ \hline \end{array}$

15. $\begin{array}{r} 5 \\ + 2 \\ \hline \end{array}$

16. $\begin{array}{r} 3 \\ + 4 \\ \hline \end{array}$

17. $\begin{array}{r} 8 \\ + 2 \\ \hline \end{array}$

18. $\begin{array}{r} 4 \\ + 1 \\ \hline \end{array}$

19. $\begin{array}{r} 6 \\ + 2 \\ \hline \end{array}$

20. $\begin{array}{r} 6 \\ + 4 \\ \hline \end{array}$

ADDITION MATH FACTS FROM 0 TO 10

1. 6
    + 4
    ───

2. 9
    + 1
    ───

3. 3
    + 5
    ───

4. 8
    + 2
    ───

5. 6
    + 3
    ───

6. 5
    + 5
    ───

7. 3
    + 7
    ───

8. 4
    + 5
    ───

9. 5
    + 3
    ───

10. 5
     + 2
     ───

11. 3
     + 4
     ───

12. 7
     + 2
     ───

13. 4
     + 1
     ───

14. 6
     + 2
     ───

15. 2
     + 4
     ───

16. 4
     + 4
     ───

17. 8
     + 1
     ───

18. 3
     + 3
     ───

19. 2
     + 5
     ───

20. 2
     + 3
     ───

ADDITION MATH FACTS FROM 0 TO 10

1. $\begin{array}{r} 1 \\ + 4 \\ \hline \end{array}$

2. $\begin{array}{r} 3 \\ + 6 \\ \hline \end{array}$

3. $\begin{array}{r} 1 \\ + 5 \\ \hline \end{array}$

4. $\begin{array}{r} 5 \\ + 2 \\ \hline \end{array}$

5. $\begin{array}{r} 2 \\ + 6 \\ \hline \end{array}$

6. $\begin{array}{r} 4 \\ + 5 \\ \hline \end{array}$

7. $\begin{array}{r} 3 \\ + 7 \\ \hline \end{array}$

8. $\begin{array}{r} 5 \\ + 5 \\ \hline \end{array}$

9. $\begin{array}{r} 3 \\ + 3 \\ \hline \end{array}$

10. $\begin{array}{r} 7 \\ + 2 \\ \hline \end{array}$

11. $\begin{array}{r} 7 \\ + 1 \\ \hline \end{array}$

12. $\begin{array}{r} 8 \\ + 1 \\ \hline \end{array}$

13. $\begin{array}{r} 4 \\ + 2 \\ \hline \end{array}$

14. $\begin{array}{r} 6 \\ + 2 \\ \hline \end{array}$

15. $\begin{array}{r} 4 \\ + 4 \\ \hline \end{array}$

16. $\begin{array}{r} 6 \\ + 4 \\ \hline \end{array}$

17. $\begin{array}{r} 8 \\ + 2 \\ \hline \end{array}$

18. $\begin{array}{r} 5 \\ + 3 \\ \hline \end{array}$

19. $\begin{array}{r} 2 \\ + 5 \\ \hline \end{array}$

20. $\begin{array}{r} 2 \\ + 3 \\ \hline \end{array}$

ADDITION MATH FACTS FROM 0 TO 10

1. 3
   + 4
   ___

2. 3
   + 3
   ___

3. 4
   + 5
   ___

4. 6
   + 2
   ___

5. 6
   + 4
   ___

6. 5
   + 5
   ___

7. 3
   + 7
   ___

8. 1
   + 5
   ___

9. 5
   + 3
   ___

10. 3
   + 2
   ___

11. 4
   + 4
   ___

12. 8
   + 1
   ___

13. 4
   + 2
   ___

14. 7
   + 2
   ___

15. 6
   + 3
   ___

16. 4
   + 3
   ___

17. 8
   + 2
   ___

18. 3
   + 5
   ___

19. 1
   + 4
   ___

20. 2
   + 5
   ___

ADDITION MATH FACTS FROM 0 TO 10

1. $\begin{array}{r} 5 \\ + 5 \\ \hline \end{array}$
2. $\begin{array}{r} 5 \\ + 2 \\ \hline \end{array}$
3. $\begin{array}{r} 5 \\ + 3 \\ \hline \end{array}$
4. $\begin{array}{r} 2 \\ + 6 \\ \hline \end{array}$
5. $\begin{array}{r} 8 \\ + 2 \\ \hline \end{array}$

6. $\begin{array}{r} 5 \\ + 4 \\ \hline \end{array}$
7. $\begin{array}{r} 3 \\ + 7 \\ \hline \end{array}$
8. $\begin{array}{r} 2 \\ + 3 \\ \hline \end{array}$
9. $\begin{array}{r} 2 \\ + 4 \\ \hline \end{array}$
10. $\begin{array}{r} 3 \\ + 4 \\ \hline \end{array}$

11. $\begin{array}{r} 4 \\ + 4 \\ \hline \end{array}$
12. $\begin{array}{r} 7 \\ + 2 \\ \hline \end{array}$
13. $\begin{array}{r} 4 \\ + 5 \\ \hline \end{array}$
14. $\begin{array}{r} 6 \\ + 2 \\ \hline \end{array}$
15. $\begin{array}{r} 6 \\ + 3 \\ \hline \end{array}$

16. $\begin{array}{r} 4 \\ + 3 \\ \hline \end{array}$
17. $\begin{array}{r} 1 \\ + 8 \\ \hline \end{array}$
18. $\begin{array}{r} 3 \\ + 5 \\ \hline \end{array}$
19. $\begin{array}{r} 2 \\ + 5 \\ \hline \end{array}$
20. $\begin{array}{r} 2 \\ + 2 \\ \hline \end{array}$

SUBTRACTION MATH FACTS FROM 0 TO 10

1. 4
    − 2

2. 5
    − 3

3. 5
    − 2

4. 7
    − 3

5. 6
    − 3

6. 10
    − 4

7. 8
    − 4

8. 10
    − 3

9. 7
    − 4

10. 9
     − 4

11. 9
     − 2

12. 10
     − 5

13. 3
     − 1

14. 8
     − 3

15. 6
     − 2

16. 7
     − 5

17. 8
     − 2

18. 10
     − 7

19. 6
     − 1

20. 6
     − 4

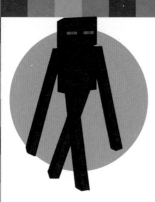

SUBTRACTION MATH FACTS FROM 0 TO 10

1. 10
 − 2

2. 7
 − 3

3. 10
 − 6

4. 6
 − 3

5. 6
 − 6

6. 10
 − 4

7. 8
 − 4

8. 10
 − 3

9. 7
 − 4

10. 5
 − 4

11. 9
 − 4

12. 10
 − 5

13. 3
 − 1

14. 8
 − 3

15. 6
 − 2

16. 7
 − 5

17. 9
 − 2

18. 10
 − 7

19. 6
 − 1

20. 6
 − 4

SUBTRACTION MATH FACTS FROM 0 TO 10

1. 10
 − 4

2. 7
 − 4

3. 8
 − 3

4. 6
 − 3

5. 6
 − 5

6. 9
 − 1

7. 9
 − 5

8. 7
 − 5

9. 10
 − 3

10. 10
 − 7

11. 9
 − 6

12. 9
 − 1

13. 5
 − 1

14. 6
 − 4

15. 8
 − 4

16. 7
 − 3

17. 8
 − 2

18. 10
 − 2

19. 10
 − 6

20. 9
 − 4

SUBTRACTION MATH FACTS FROM 0 TO 10

1. $\begin{array}{r} 10 \\ -\ 8 \\ \hline \end{array}$

2. $\begin{array}{r} 7 \\ -\ 5 \\ \hline \end{array}$

3. $\begin{array}{r} 8 \\ -\ 5 \\ \hline \end{array}$

4. $\begin{array}{r} 6 \\ -\ 3 \\ \hline \end{array}$

5. $\begin{array}{r} 6 \\ -\ 5 \\ \hline \end{array}$

6. $\begin{array}{r} 10 \\ -\ 6 \\ \hline \end{array}$

7. $\begin{array}{r} 8 \\ -\ 6 \\ \hline \end{array}$

8. $\begin{array}{r} 8 \\ -\ 3 \\ \hline \end{array}$

9. $\begin{array}{r} 7 \\ -\ 2 \\ \hline \end{array}$

10. $\begin{array}{r} 10 \\ -\ 7 \\ \hline \end{array}$

11. $\begin{array}{r} 9 \\ -\ 6 \\ \hline \end{array}$

12. $\begin{array}{r} 7 \\ -\ 3 \\ \hline \end{array}$

13. $\begin{array}{r} 9 \\ -\ 1 \\ \hline \end{array}$

14. $\begin{array}{r} 9 \\ -\ 4 \\ \hline \end{array}$

15. $\begin{array}{r} 8 \\ -\ 4 \\ \hline \end{array}$

16. $\begin{array}{r} 7 \\ -\ 4 \\ \hline \end{array}$

17. $\begin{array}{r} 8 \\ -\ 2 \\ \hline \end{array}$

18. $\begin{array}{r} 10 \\ -\ 4 \\ \hline \end{array}$

19. $\begin{array}{r} 10 \\ -\ 2 \\ \hline \end{array}$

20. $\begin{array}{r} 6 \\ -\ 4 \\ \hline \end{array}$

SUBTRACTION MATH FACTS FROM 0 TO 10

1. 9
   − 8

2. 8
   − 6

3. 7
   − 5

4. 8
   − 3

5. 8
   − 8

6. 9
   − 7

7. 8
   − 4

8. 9
   − 5

9. 6
   − 6

10. 7
   − 6

11. 7
   − 7

12. 8
   − 7

13. 9
   − 9

14. 10
   − 8

15. 9
   − 6

16. 8
   − 5

17. 8
   − 8

18. 10
   − 5

19. 6
   − 3

20. 4
   − 2

ADDITION MATH FACTS FROM 0 TO 20

1. $\begin{array}{r} 9 \\ +\ 7 \\ \hline \end{array}$ 2. $\begin{array}{r} 8 \\ +\ 8 \\ \hline \end{array}$ 3. $\begin{array}{r} 9 \\ +10 \\ \hline \end{array}$ 4. $\begin{array}{r} 4 \\ +\ 8 \\ \hline \end{array}$ 5. $\begin{array}{r} 9 \\ +\ 6 \\ \hline \end{array}$

6. $\begin{array}{r} 6 \\ +\ 7 \\ \hline \end{array}$ 7. $\begin{array}{r} 8 \\ +\ 7 \\ \hline \end{array}$ 8. $\begin{array}{r} 9 \\ +\ 9 \\ \hline \end{array}$ 9. $\begin{array}{r} 4 \\ +\ 9 \\ \hline \end{array}$ 10. $\begin{array}{r} 7 \\ +\ 7 \\ \hline \end{array}$

11. $\begin{array}{r} 5 \\ +\ 9 \\ \hline \end{array}$ 12. $\begin{array}{r} 6 \\ +\ 8 \\ \hline \end{array}$ 13. $\begin{array}{r} 7 \\ +\ 5 \\ \hline \end{array}$ 14. $\begin{array}{r} 8 \\ +\ 3 \\ \hline \end{array}$ 15. $\begin{array}{r} 6 \\ +\ 6 \\ \hline \end{array}$

16. $\begin{array}{r} 4 \\ +\ 7 \\ \hline \end{array}$ 17. $\begin{array}{r} 8 \\ +\ 5 \\ \hline \end{array}$ 18. $\begin{array}{r} 7 \\ +\ 8 \\ \hline \end{array}$ 19. $\begin{array}{r} 5 \\ +\ 6 \\ \hline \end{array}$ 20. $\begin{array}{r} 7 \\ +\ 6 \\ \hline \end{array}$

ADDITION MATH FACTS FROM 0 TO 20

1. 9
   + 2

2. 8
   + 3

3. 7
   + 4

4. 6
   + 5

5. 5
   + 7

6. 6
   + 7

7. 8
   + 7

8. 9
   + 9

9. 4
   + 9

10. 7
    + 7

11. 5
    + 9

12. 6
    + 8

13. 7
    + 5

14. 8
    + 4

15. 6
    + 6

16. 4
    + 7

17. 8
    + 5

18. 4
    + 8

19. 5
    + 6

20. 7
    + 6

ADDITION MATH FACTS FROM 0 TO 20

1. 9
   + 6

2. 8
   + 3

3. 7
   + 4

4. 6
   + 5

5. 7
   + 7

6. 6
   + 7

7. 8
   + 7

8. 9
   + 9

9. 4
   + 9

10. 5
    + 7

11. 5
    + 9

12. 6
    + 8

13. 7
    + 5

14. 8
    + 4

15. 3
    + 9

16. 2
    + 9

17. 8
    + 5

18. 4
    + 8

19. 8
    + 6

20. 6
    + 6

ADDITION MATH FACTS FROM 0 TO 20

1. 3
   + 8
   ___

2. 2
   + 9
   ___

3. 4
   + 7
   ___

4. 5
   + 7
   ___

5. 6
   + 6
   ___

6. 8
   + 6
   ___

7. 8
   + 5
   ___

8. 7
   + 8
   ___

9. 9
   + 9
   ___

10. 4
    + 8
    ___

11. 5
    + 9
    ___

12. 6
    + 8
    ___

13. 7
    + 9
    ___

14. 8
    + 4
    ___

15. 9
    + 3
    ___

16. 8
    + 7
    ___

17. 8
    + 8
    ___

18. 4
    + 9
    ___

19. 8
    + 3
    ___

20. 5
    + 6
    ___

ADDITION MATH FACTS FROM 0 TO 20

1. 7
+ 5

2. 7
+ 9

3. 8
+ 7

4. 9
+ 7

5. 9
+ 9

6. 6
+ 6

7. 8
+ 6

8. 4
+ 7

9. 9
+ 3

10. 4
+ 8

11. 5
+ 6

12. 6
+ 7

13. 8
+ 8

14. 8
+ 4

15. 8
+ 3

16. 9
+ 4

17. 7
+ 8

18. 3
+ 9

19. 3
+ 8

20. 5
+ 8

ADDITION MATH FACTS FROM 0 TO 20

1. 8
  + 5

2. 3
  + 9

3. 8
  + 8

4. 9
  + 8

5. 7
  + 6

6. 8
  + 6

7. 6
  + 6

8. 8
  + 7

9. 7
  + 5

10. 4
   + 8

11. 5
   + 6

12. 4
   + 7

13. 3
   + 8

14. 7
   + 4

15. 9
   + 3

16. 9
   + 9

17. 10
   + 6

18. 7
   + 9

19. 12
   + 8

20. 5
   + 8

ADDITION MATH FACTS FROM 0 TO 20

1. 7
   + 7

2. 9
   + 7

3. 10
   + 8

4. 11
   + 7

5. 12
   + 3

6. 13
   + 5

7. 14
   + 2

8. 16
   + 2

9.   2
   +10

10.   7
   +11

11.   4
   +13

12.   2
   +16

13.   1
   +17

14.   8
   + 7

15. 10
   + 3

16. 11
   + 4

17. 12
   + 6

18. 13
   + 4

19. 14
   + 4

20. 15
   + 3

ADDITION MATH FACTS FROM 0 TO 20

1. 17
   + 1
   ———

2.   4
   +11
   ———

3.   5
   +12
   ———

4.   3
   +14
   ———

5.   2
   +15
   ———

6. 10
   + 9
   ———

7.   8
   +11
   ———

8. 11
   + 7
   ———

9.   7
   +12
   ———

10. 11
   + 9
   ———

11.   8
   +12
   ———

12. 10
   + 8
   ———

13.   5
   +13
   ———

14. 12
   + 6
   ———

15.   7
   +13
   ———

16.   5
   +14
   ———

17. 15
   + 3
   ———

18. 16
   + 4
   ———

19. 17
   + 2
   ———

20. 19
   + 1
   ———

ADDITION MATH FACTS FROM 0 TO 20

1. 14
   + 2

2. 4
   + 15

3. 3
   + 12

4. 4
   + 14

5. 3
   + 15

6. 11
   + 9

7. 7
   + 11

8. 13
   + 7

9. 6
   + 12

10. 8
   + 9

11. 5
   + 12

12. 14
   + 3

13. 5
   + 14

14. 12
   + 7

15. 3
   + 13

16. 2
   + 16

17. 15
   + 5

18. 16
   + 4

19. 17
   + 2

20. 12
   + 5

ADDITION MATH FACTS FROM 0 TO 20

1. 13
   + 4

2. 4
   +15

3. 3
   +12

4. 6
   +14

5. 3
   +15

6. 7
   + 9

7. 7
   +11

8. 13
   + 6

9. 6
   + 12

10. 8
    + 9

11. 4
    +12

12. 14
    + 5

13. 3
    +14

14. 12
    + 7

15. 3
    +13

16. 4
    + 9

17. 15
    + 5

18. 16
    + 3

19. 13
    + 2

20. 13
    + 5

SUBTRACTION MATH FACTS FROM 0 TO 20

1. 13
− 6

2. 12
− 8

3. 11
− 7

4. 14
− 7

5. 15
− 7

6. 12
− 6

7. 16
− 8

8. 15
− 9

9. 17
− 5

10. 16
− 5

11. 14
− 6

12. 15
− 5

13. 17
− 8

14. 12
− 5

15. 12
− 4

16. 13
− 7

17. 12
− 7

18. 11
− 4

19. 11
− 6

20. 12
− 3

SUBTRACTION MATH FACTS FROM 0 TO 20

1. 15
  − 6

2. 14
  − 8

3. 12
  − 7

4. 11
  − 7

5. 14
  − 7

6. 13
  − 5

7. 16
  − 9

8. 15
  − 8

9. 17
  − 6

10. 16
  − 8

11. 16
  − 6

12. 14
  − 5

13. 17
  − 9

14. 12
  − 5

15. 12
  − 3

16. 13
  − 2

17. 12
  − 8

18. 11
  − 5

19. 11
  − 2

20. 12
  − 6

SUBTRACTION MATH FACTS FROM 0 TO 20

1. 14 − 6

2. 14 − 5

3. 17 − 9

4. 12 − 5

5. 12 − 3

6. 13 − 7

7. 12 − 8

8. 11 − 7

9. 11 − 5

10. 17 − 10

11. 15 − 6

12. 15 − 8

13. 12 − 7

14. 11 − 2

15. 14 − 7

16. 13 − 6

17. 16 − 9

18. 15 − 7

19. 17 − 6

20. 16 − 5

SUBTRACTION MATH FACTS FROM 0 TO 20

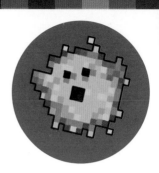

1. 16
    − 3

2. 13
    − 3

3. 14
    − 2

4. 15
    − 2

5. 17
    − 6

6. 12
    − 5

7. 14
    − 7

8. 18
    − 9

9. 16
    − 9

10. 11
    − 6

11. 15
    − 7

12. 15
    − 9

13. 13
    − 6

14. 14
    − 6

15. 17
    − 9

16. 14
    − 8

17. 16
    − 8

18. 12
    − 4

19. 12
    − 7

20. 11
    − 8

SUBTRACTION MATH FACTS FROM 0 TO 20

1. 11
    − 3

2. 13
    − 3

3. 14
    − 6

4. 15
    − 8

5. 17
    − 6

6. 12
    − 3

7. 12
    − 4

8. 16
    − 9

9. 17
    − 9

10. 11
    − 6

11. 15
    − 9

12. 14
    − 7

13. 13
    − 6

14. 12
    − 6

15. 17
    − 8

16. 14
    − 8

17. 16
    − 8

18. 12
    − 8

19. 12
    − 5

20. 11
    − 10

SUBTRACTION MATH FACTS FROM 0 TO 20

1. 20
   − 3

2. 18
   − 6

3. 17
   − 4

4. 15
   − 10

5. 20
   − 4

6. 17
   − 5

7. 16
   − 3

8. 19
   − 4

9. 20
   − 7

10. 19
    − 5

11. 16
    − 7

12. 20
    − 6

13. 20
    − 2

14. 15
    − 3

15. 17
    − 3

16. 14
    − 4

17. 19
    − 3

18. 20
    − 8

19. 15
    − 4

20. 20
    − 11

SUBTRACTION MATH FACTS FROM 0 TO 20

1. 20
    − 4

2. 19
    − 6

3. 16
    − 5

4. 18
    − 10

5. 20
    − 5

6. 17
    − 3

7. 16
    − 4

8. 19
    − 2

9. 20
    − 3

10. 19
    − 4

11. 16
    − 3

12. 20
    − 7

13. 20
    − 1

14. 15
    − 2

15. 17
    − 7

16. 15
    − 4

17. 19
    − 3

18. 18
    − 5

19. 15
    − 3

20. 20
    − 9

SUBTRACTION MATH FACTS FROM 0 TO 20

1. 16
  − 4

2. 13
  − 6

3. 20
  −10

4. 18
  − 9

5. 20
  − 3

6. 17
  − 5

7. 16
  − 8

8. 19
  − 8

9. 14
  − 3

10. 18
  − 4

11. 16
  − 1

12. 20
  − 4

13. 15
  − 4

14. 15
  − 8

15. 17
  − 8

16. 15
  − 5

17. 19
  − 5

18. 18
  − 8

19. 12
  − 4

20. 20
  − 7

SUBTRACTION MATH FACTS FROM 0 TO 20

1. 16
    − 7

2. 14
    − 6

3. 13
    − 5

4. 18
    − 5

5. 20
    − 5

6. 17
    − 6

7. 16
    − 4

8. 17
    − 8

9. 19
    − 3

10. 18
    − 15

11. 16
    −10

12. 20
    − 7

13. 15
    −11

14. 14
    − 8

15. 17
    − 7

16. 15
    − 8

17. 19
    − 2

18. 18
    − 6

19. 12
    − 9

20. 20
    − 3

SUBTRACTION MATH FACTS FROM 0 TO 20

1. $\begin{array}{r} 16 \\ -\ 8 \\ \hline \end{array}$

2. $\begin{array}{r} 14 \\ -\ 9 \\ \hline \end{array}$

3. $\begin{array}{r} 13 \\ -\ 3 \\ \hline \end{array}$

4. $\begin{array}{r} 12 \\ -\ 5 \\ \hline \end{array}$

5. $\begin{array}{r} 11 \\ -\ 5 \\ \hline \end{array}$

6. $\begin{array}{r} 11 \\ -\ 4 \\ \hline \end{array}$

7. $\begin{array}{r} 16 \\ -\ 7 \\ \hline \end{array}$

8. $\begin{array}{r} 17 \\ -\ 8 \\ \hline \end{array}$

9. $\begin{array}{r} 15 \\ -\ 9 \\ \hline \end{array}$

10. $\begin{array}{r} 18 \\ -10 \\ \hline \end{array}$

11. $\begin{array}{r} 16 \\ -\ 5 \\ \hline \end{array}$

12. $\begin{array}{r} 20 \\ -10 \\ \hline \end{array}$

13. $\begin{array}{r} 15 \\ -\ 5 \\ \hline \end{array}$

14. $\begin{array}{r} 14 \\ -\ 6 \\ \hline \end{array}$

15. $\begin{array}{r} 17 \\ -\ 9 \\ \hline \end{array}$

16. $\begin{array}{r} 15 \\ -\ 7 \\ \hline \end{array}$

17. $\begin{array}{r} 13 \\ -\ 6 \\ \hline \end{array}$

18. $\begin{array}{r} 14 \\ -\ 8 \\ \hline \end{array}$

19. $\begin{array}{r} 12 \\ -\ 4 \\ \hline \end{array}$

20. $\begin{array}{r} 13 \\ -\ 7 \\ \hline \end{array}$

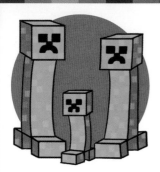

MIXED ADDITION & SUBTRACTION FROM 0 TO 20

1. 3
  + 8

2. 16
  − 5

3. 4
  + 7

4. 18
  − 9

5. 6
  + 6

6. 8
  − 6

7. 8
  + 5

8. 7
  − 7

9. 9
  + 9

10. 12
  − 8

11. 5
  + 9

12. 15
  − 7

13. 7
  + 9

14. 8
  − 4

15. 9
  + 3

16. 8
  − 7

17. 8
  + 8

18. 12
  − 9

19. 8
  + 3

20. 11
  − 6

MIXED ADDITION & SUBTRACTION FROM 0 TO 20

1. 8
  + 5

2. 11
  − 3

3. 8
  + 7

4. 17
  − 8

5. 7
  + 6

6. 13
  − 6

7. 6
  + 6

8. 12
  − 5

9. 7
  + 5

10. 14
  − 8

11. 5
  + 6

12. 14
  − 7

13. 3
  + 8

14. 17
  − 9

15. 9
  + 3

16. 9
  + 9

17. 12
  + 8

18. 7
  + 9

19. 12
  − 3

20. 5
  + 8

MIXED ADDITION & SUBTRACTION FROM 0 TO 20

1. 9
  + 7

2. 18
  − 8

3. 20
  − 5

4. 12
  + 8

5. 9
  + 6

6. 8
  + 7

7. 16
  − 7

8. 20
  − 9

9. 4
  + 7

10. 9
  + 5

11. 15
  − 9

12. 6
  + 8

13. 7
  + 6

14. 13
  − 6

15. 6
  + 6

16. 14
  − 6

17. 18
  − 9

18. 7
  + 5

19. 5
  + 6

20. 7
  + 7

MIXED ADDITION & SUBTRACTION FROM 0 TO 20

1. 9
    + 2

2. 8
    + 3

3. 17
    - 9

4. 16
    - 5

5. 9
    + 7

6. 12
    - 5

7. 5
    + 7

8. 9
    + 9

9. 12
    - 4

10. 7
    + 7

11. 5
    + 9

12. 16
    - 8

13. 7
    + 6

14. 8
    + 4

15. 14
    - 8

16. 4
    + 7

17. 12
    - 9

18. 4
    + 9

19. 15
    - 7

20. 7
    + 8

MYSTERY NUMBER ADDITION

Fill in the missing number to complete the equation.

Examples:

1. 3
    + [4]
    ___
    7

2. [6]
    + 4
    ___
    10

3. 6
    + [ ]
    ___
    8

4. 5
    + [ ]
    ___
    8

5. 4
    + [ ]
    ___
    8

6. [ ]
    + 5
    ___
    9

7. 5
    + [ ]
    ___
    10

8. 2
    + 7
    ___
    [ ]

9. [ ]
    + 6
    ___
    9

10. 2
    + [ ]
    ___
    5

11. [ ]
    + 3
    ___
    6

12. 7
    + [ ]
    ___
    10

13. 4
    + 4
    ___
    [ ]

14. 9
    + [ ]
    ___
    10

15. [ ]
    + 1
    ___
    8

16. [ ]
    + 2
    ___
    6

17. 2
    + [ ]
    ___
    7

18. 2
    + 4
    ___
    [ ]

19. [ ]
    + 3
    ___
    9

20. 8
    + [ ]
    ___
    10

MYSTERY NUMBER ADDITION

Fill in the missing number to complete the equation.

1. 13
    + ☐
    ———
      20

2. ☐
    + 4
    ———
      16

3. 6
    + ☐
    ———
      14

4. 5
    + ☐
    ———
      13

5. 4
    + ☐
    ———
      12

6. ☐
    + 5
    ———
      12

7. 5
    + ☐
    ———
      11

8. 2
    + 7
    ———
      ☐

9. ☐
    + 3
    ———
      12

10. 2
    + ☐
    ———
      10

11. ☐
    + 3
    ———
      12

12. 7
    + 7
    ———
      ☐

13. 4
    +16
    ———
      ☐

14. 9
    + ☐
    ———
      14

15. ☐
    + 7
    ———
      12

16. ☐
    + 7
    ———
      13

17. 6
    + ☐
    ———
      12

18. 8
    + 6
    ———
      ☐

19. ☐
    + 6
    ———
      15

20. 8
    + ☐
    ———
      18

47

MYSTERY NUMBER SUBTRACTION

Fill in the missing number to complete the equation.

1.
$$\begin{array}{r} 10 \\ - \boxed{} \\ \hline 7 \end{array}$$

2.
$$\begin{array}{r} \boxed{} \\ - \ 4 \\ \hline 4 \end{array}$$

3.
$$\begin{array}{r} 6 \\ - \boxed{} \\ \hline 3 \end{array}$$

4.
$$\begin{array}{r} 8 \\ - \boxed{} \\ \hline 5 \end{array}$$

5.
$$\begin{array}{r} 4 \\ - \boxed{} \\ \hline 4 \end{array}$$

6.
$$\begin{array}{r} \boxed{} \\ - \ 5 \\ \hline 4 \end{array}$$

7.
$$\begin{array}{r} 5 \\ - \boxed{} \\ \hline 3 \end{array}$$

8.
$$\begin{array}{r} 2 \\ - \ 1 \\ \hline \boxed{} \end{array}$$

9.
$$\begin{array}{r} \boxed{} \\ - \ 6 \\ \hline 4 \end{array}$$

10.
$$\begin{array}{r} 5 \\ - \boxed{} \\ \hline 1 \end{array}$$

11.
$$\begin{array}{r} \boxed{} \\ - \ 2 \\ \hline 8 \end{array}$$

12.
$$\begin{array}{r} 7 \\ - \boxed{} \\ \hline 2 \end{array}$$

13.
$$\begin{array}{r} 7 \\ - \ 4 \\ \hline \boxed{} \end{array}$$

14.
$$\begin{array}{r} 9 \\ - \boxed{} \\ \hline 5 \end{array}$$

15.
$$\begin{array}{r} \boxed{} \\ - \ 1 \\ \hline 8 \end{array}$$

16.
$$\begin{array}{r} \boxed{} \\ - \ 2 \\ \hline 6 \end{array}$$

17.
$$\begin{array}{r} 9 \\ - \boxed{} \\ \hline 7 \end{array}$$

18.
$$\begin{array}{r} 4 \\ - \ 2 \\ \hline \boxed{} \end{array}$$

19.
$$\begin{array}{r} \boxed{} \\ - \ 2 \\ \hline 8 \end{array}$$

20.
$$\begin{array}{r} 8 \\ - \boxed{} \\ \hline 2 \end{array}$$

MYSTERY NUMBER SUBTRACTION

Fill in the missing number to complete the equation.

1.   13
   - ☐
   ____
    10

2.   ☐
   - 4
   ____
    16

3.   16
   - ☐
   ____
    8

4.   15
   - ☐
   ____
    10

5.   14
   - ☐
   ____
    12

6.   ☐
   - 5
   ____
    6

7.   12
   - ☐
   ____
    7

8.   12
   - 9
   ____
    ☐

9.   ☐
   - 6
   ____
    11

10.   13
   - ☐
   ____
    8

11.   ☐
   - 3
   ____
    12

12.   17
   - 7
   ____
    ☐

13.   16
   - 4
   ____
    ☐

14.   19
   - ☐
   ____
    15

15.   ☐
   - 3
   ____
    11

16.   ☐
   - 6
   ____
    7

17.   18
   - ☐
   ____
    13

18.   18
   - 6
   ____
    ☐

19.   ☐
   - 6
   ____
    14

20.   18
   - ☐
   ____
    9

DOUBLE-DIGIT ADDITION FROM 0-100

1. 30
+50

2. 20
+70

3. 60
+13

4. 34
+51

5. 16
+23

6. 40
+50

7. 23
+53

8. 25
+14

9. 40
+58

10. 40
+30

11. 30
+28

12. 24
+12

13. 35
+13

14. 20
+60

15. 17
+22

16. 42
+50

17. 23
+12

18. 23
+54

19. 50
+18

20. 83
+16

DOUBLE-DIGIT ADDITION FROM 0-100

1. 52
   +13

2. 25
   +14

3. 20
   +71

4. 60
   +32

5. 24
   +43

6. 27
   +31

7. 45
   +54

8. 66
   +33

9. 46
   +53

10. 38
    +21

11. 70
    +22

12. 62
    +24

13. 78
    +11

14. 53
    +15

15. 74
    +24

16. 27
    +51

17. 30
    +32

18. 67
    +12

19. 23
    +45

20. 42
    +44

DOUBLE-DIGIT ADDITION FROM 0-100

1. 62
    +13
    ———

2. 28
    +10
    ———

3. 22
    +71
    ———

4. 50
    +34
    ———

5. 27
    +42
    ———

6. 26
    +33
    ———

7. 48
    +50
    ———

8. 65
    +33
    ———

9. 36
    +53
    ———

10. 27
    +31
    ———

11. 20
    +72
    ———

12. 42
    +24
    ———

13. 51
    +11
    ———

14. 73
    +15
    ———

15. 70
    +20
    ———

16. 37
    +51
    ———

17. 50
    +32
    ———

18. 33
    +14
    ———

19. 63
    +25
    ———

20. 42
    +17
    ———

DOUBLE-DIGIT ADDITION FROM 0-100

1. 32
   +51

2. 27
   +12

3. 21
   +75

4. 40
   +24

5. 87
   +10

6. 46
   +33

7. 38
   +61

8. 60
   +39

9. 31
   +54

10. 90
   +10

11. 30
   +52

12. 44
   +14

13. 56
   +31

14. 33
   +15

15. 40
   +20

16. 38
   +31

17. 30
   +42

18. 53
   +14

19. 64
   +25

20. 42
   +15

DOUBLE-DIGIT SUBTRACTION FROM 0-100

1. 88
    −33

2. 77
    −12

3. 29
    −17

4. 40
    − 24

5. 87
    − 10

6. 49
    −33

7. 48
    − 21

8. 60
    −30

9. 81
    − 51

10. 90
    − 10

11. 50
    − 20

12. 94
    − 14

13. 66
    − 32

14. 53
    −13

15. 45
    − 20

16. 38
    −31

17. 87
    −42

18. 53
    − 12

19. 64
    − 22

20. 42
    − 12

DOUBLE-DIGIT SUBTRACTION FROM 0-100

1. 56
   −32

2. 72
   −12

3. 39
   −14

4. 44
   −21

5. 77
   −10

6. 86
   −33

7. 28
   −21

8. 60
   −30

9. 67
   −55

10. 80
   −10

11. 70
   −40

12. 56
   −12

13. 67
   −34

14. 87
   −13

15. 75
   −10

16. 35
   −31

17. 97
   −40

18. 59
   −12

19. 74
   −11

20. 49
   −19

DOUBLE-DIGIT SUBTRACTION FROM 0-100

1. 86
    − 42

2. 67
    − 12

3. 93
    − 11

4. 74
    − 21

5. 57
    − 14

6. 26
    − 13

7. 77
    − 51

8. 54
    − 30

9. 67
    − 40

10. 88
    − 22

11. 33
    − 11

12. 89
    − 67

13. 37
    − 34

14. 86
    − 13

15. 39
    − 14

16. 63
    − 30

17. 97
    − 27

18. 49
    − 23

19. 34
    − 21

20. 87
    − 15

DOUBLE-DIGIT SUBTRACTION FROM 0-100

1. 97
  − 32

2. 54
  − 12

3. 62
  − 21

4. 84
  − 24

5. 76
  − 14

6. 28
  − 13

7. 87
  − 54

8. 57
  − 20

9. 37
  − 15

10. 58
  − 22

11. 73
  − 21

12. 49
  − 25

13. 87
  − 64

14. 96
  − 33

15. 35
  − 14

16. 68
  − 30

17. 27
  − 17

18. 99
  − 27

19. 75
  − 25

20. 86
  − 22

ANSWERS

PAGE 8

1. 7
2. 6
3. 3
4. 10
5. 8
6. 6
7. 4
8. 3
9. 4
10. 10
11. 8
12. 0
13. 2
14. 7
15. 9
16. 9
17. 1
18. 3
19. 5
20. 5

PAGE 9

1. 8
2. 6
3. 2
4. 10
5. 7
6. 4
7. 9
8. 3
9. 6
10. 10
11. 7
12. 0
13. 3
14. 8
15. 4
16. 9
17. 5
18. 3
19. 1
20. 5

PAGE 10

1. 7
2. 4
3. 1
4. 8
5. 6
6. 6
7. 2
8. 3
9. 4
10. 9
11. 8
12. 0
13. 4
14. 5
15. 7
16. 9
17. 1
18. 2
19. 5
20. 3

PAGE 11

1. 8
2. 0
3. 8
4. 5
5. 7
6. 7
7. 1
8. 0
9. 5
10. 3
11. 6
12. 4
13. 2
14. 9
15. 6
16. 9
17. 4
18. 3
19. 1
20. 2

PAGE 12

1. 6
2. 8
3. 10
4. 9
5. 9
6. 8
7. 9
8. 6
9. 7
10. 5
11. 10
12. 10
13. 9
14. 8
15. 7
16. 7
17. 10
18. 5
19. 8
20. 10

PAGE 13

1. 10
2. 10
3. 8
4. 10
5. 9
6. 10
7. 10
8. 9
9. 8
10. 7
11. 7
12. 9
13. 5
14. 8
15. 6
16. 8
17. 9
18. 6
19. 7
20. 5

PAGE 14

1. 5
2. 9
3. 6
4. 7
5. 8
6. 9
7. 10
8. 10
9. 6
10. 9
11. 8
12. 9
13. 6
14. 8
15. 8
16. 10
17. 10
18. 8
19. 7
20. 5

PAGE 15

1. 7
2. 6
3. 9
4. 8
5. 10
6. 10
7. 10
8. 6
9. 8
10. 5
11. 8
12. 9
13. 6
14. 9
15. 9
16. 7
17. 10
18. 8
19. 5
20. 7

PAGE 16

1. 10
2. 7
3. 8
4. 8
5. 10
6. 9
7. 10
8. 5
9. 6
10. 7
11. 8
12. 9
13. 9
14. 8
15. 9
16. 7
17. 9
18. 8
19. 7
20. 4

PAGE 17

1. 2
2. 2
3. 3
4. 4
5. 3
6. 6
7. 4
8. 7
9. 3
10. 5
11. 7
12. 5
13. 2
14. 5
15. 4
16. 2
17. 6
18. 3
19. 5
20. 2

PAGE 18

1. 8
2. 4
3. 4
4. 3
5. 0
6. 6
7. 4
8. 7
9. 3
10. 1
11. 5
12. 5
13. 2
14. 5
15. 4
16. 2
17. 7
18. 3
19. 5
20. 2

PAGE 19

1. 6
2. 3
3. 5
4. 3
5. 1
6. 8
7. 4
8. 2
9. 7
10. 3
11. 3
12. 8
13. 4
14. 2
15. 4
16. 4
17. 6
18. 8
19. 4
20. 5

PAGE 20

1. 2
2. 2
3. 3
4. 3
5. 1
6. 4
7. 2
8. 5
9. 5
10. 3
11. 3
12. 4
13. 8
14. 5
15. 4
16. 3
17. 6
18. 6
19. 8
20. 2

PAGE 21

1. 1
2. 2
3. 2
4. 5
5. 0
6. 2
7. 4
8. 4
9. 0
10. 1
11. 0
12. 1
13. 0
14. 2
15. 3
16. 3
17. 0
18. 5
19. 3
20. 2

PAGE 22

1. 16
2. 16
3. 19
4. 12
5. 15
6. 13
7. 15
8. 18
9. 13
10. 14
11. 14
12. 14
13. 12
14. 11
15. 12
16. 11
17. 13
18. 15
19. 11
20. 13

PAGE 23

1. 11
2. 11
3. 11
4. 11
5. 12
6. 13
7. 15
8. 18
9. 13
10. 14
11. 14
12. 14
13. 12
14. 12
15. 12
16. 11
17. 13
18. 12
19. 11
20. 13

PAGE 24

1. 15
2. 11
3. 11
4. 11
5. 14
6. 13
7. 15
8. 18
9. 13
10. 12
11. 14
12. 14
13. 12
14. 12
15. 12
16. 11
17. 13
18. 12
19. 14
20. 12

PAGE 25

1. 11
2. 11
3. 11
4. 12
5. 12
6. 14
7. 13
8. 15
9. 18
10. 12
11. 14
12. 14
13. 16
14. 12
15. 12
16. 15
17. 16
18. 13
19. 11
20. 11

PAGE 26

1. 12
2. 16
3. 15
4. 16
5. 18
6. 12
7. 14
8. 11
9. 12
10. 12
11. 11
12. 13
13. 16
14. 12
15. 11
16. 13
17. 15
18. 12
19. 11
20. 13

PAGE 27

1. 13
2. 12
3. 16
4. 17
5. 13
6. 14
7. 12
8. 15
9. 12
10. 12
11. 11
12. 11
13. 11
14. 11
15. 12
16. 18
17. 16
18. 16
19. 20
20. 13

PAGE 34

1. 8
2. 9
3. 8
4. 7
5. 9
6. 6
7. 4
8. 4
9. 6
10. 7
11. 9
12. 7
13. 5
14. 9
15. 7
16. 7
17. 7
18. 8
19. 11
20. 11

PAGE 35

1. 13
2. 10
3. 12
4. 13
5. 11
6. 7
7. 7
8. 9
9. 7
10. 5
11. 8
12. 6
13. 7
14. 8
15. 8
16. 6
17. 8
18. 8
19. 5
20. 3

PAGE 36

1. 8
2. 10
3. 8
4. 7
5. 11
6. 9
7. 8
8. 7
9. 8
10. 5
11. 6
12. 7
13. 7
14. 6
15. 9
16. 6
17. 8
18. 4
19. 7
20. 1

PAGE 37

1. 17
2. 12
3. 13
4. 5
5. 16
6. 12
7. 13
8. 15
9. 13
10. 14
11. 9
12. 14
13. 18
14. 12
15. 14
16. 10
17. 16
18. 12
19. 11
20. 9

PAGE 38

1. 16
2. 13
3. 11
4. 8
5. 15
6. 14
7. 12
8. 17
9. 17
10. 15
11. 13
12. 13
13. 19
14. 13
15. 10
16. 11
17. 16
18. 13
19. 12
20. 11

PAGE 39

1. 12
2. 7
3. 10
4. 9
5. 17
6. 12
7. 8
8. 11
9. 11
10. 14
11. 15
12. 16
13. 11
14. 7
15. 9
16. 10
17. 14
18. 10
19. 8
20. 13

PAGE 40

1. 9
2. 8
3. 8
4. 13
5. 15
6. 11
7. 12
8. 9
9. 16
10. 3
11. 6
12. 13
13. 4
14. 6
15. 10
16. 7
17. 17
18. 12
19. 3
20. 17

PAGE 41

1. 8
2. 5
3. 10
4. 7
5. 6
6. 7
7. 9
8. 9
9. 6
10. 8
11. 11
12. 10
13. 10
14. 8
15. 8
16. 8
17. 7
18. 6
19. 8
20. 6

PAGE 42

1. 11
2. 11
3. 11
4. 9
5. 12
6. 2
7. 13
8. 0
9. 18
10. 4
11. 14
12. 8
13. 16
14. 4
15. 12
16. 1
17. 16
18. 3
19. 11
20. 5

PAGE 43

1. 13
2. 8
3. 15
4. 9
5. 13
6. 7
7. 12
8. 7
9. 12
10. 6
11. 11
12. 7
13. 11
14. 8
15. 12
16. 18
17. 20
18. 16
19. 9
20. 13

PAGE 44

1. 16
2. 10
3. 15
4. 20
5. 15
6. 15
7. 9
8. 11
9. 11
10. 14
11. 6
12. 14
13. 13
14. 7
15. 12
16. 8
17. 9
18. 12
19. 11
20. 14

PAGE 45

1. 11
2. 11
3. 8
4. 11
5. 16
6. 7
7. 12
8. 18
9. 8
10. 14
11. 14
12. 8
13. 13
14. 12
15. 6
16. 11
17. 3
18. 13
19. 8
20. 15

PAGE 46

1. 4
2. 6
3. 2
4. 3
5. 4
6. 4
7. 5
8. 9
9. 3
10. 3
11. 3
12. 3
13. 8
14. 1
15. 7
16. 4
17. 5
18. 6
19. 6
20. 2

PAGE 47

1. 7
2. 12
3. 8
4. 8
5. 8
6. 7
7. 6
8. 9
9. 9
10. 8
11. 9
12. 14
13. 20
14. 5
15. 5
16. 6
17. 6
18. 14
19. 9
20. 10

PAGE 48

1. 3
2. 8
3. 3
4. 3
5. 0
6. 9
7. 2
8. 1
9. 10
10. 4
11. 10
12. 5
13. 3
14. 4
15. 9
16. 8
17. 2
18. 2
19. 10
20. 6

PAGE 49

1. 3
2. 20
3. 8
4. 5
5. 2
6. 11
7. 5
8. 3
9. 17
10. 5
11. 15
12. 10
13. 12
14. 4
15. 14
16. 13
17. 5
18. 12
19. 20
20. 9

PAGE 50

1. 80
2. 90
3. 73
4. 85
5. 39
6. 90
7. 76
8. 39
9. 98
10. 70
11. 58
12. 36
13. 48
14. 80
15. 39
16. 92
17. 35
18. 77
19. 68
20. 99

PAGE 51

1. 65
2. 39
3. 91
4. 92
5. 67
6. 58
7. 99
8. 99
9. 99
10. 59
11. 92
12. 86
13. 89
14. 68
15. 98
16. 78
17. 62
18. 79
19. 68
20. 86

PAGE 52

1. 75
2. 38
3. 93
4. 84
5. 69
6. 59
7. 98
8. 98
9. 89
10. 58
11. 92
12. 66
13. 66
14. 88
15. 90
16. 88
17. 82
18. 47
19. 88
20. 59

PAGE 53

1. 83
2. 39
3. 96
4. 64
5. 97
6. 79
7. 99
8. 99
9. 85
10. 100
11. 82
12. 58
13. 87
14. 48
15. 60
16. 69
17. 72
18. 67
19. 89
20. 57

PAGE 54

1. 55
2. 65
3. 12
4. 16
5. 77
6. 16
7. 27
8. 30
9. 30
10. 80
11. 30
12. 80
13. 34
14. 40
15. 25
16. 7
17. 45
18. 41
19. 42
20. 30

PAGE 55

1. 24
2. 60
3. 25
4. 23
5. 67
6. 53
7. 7
8. 30
9. 12
10. 70
11. 30
12. 44
13. 33
14. 74
15. 65
16. 4
17. 57
18. 47
19. 63
20. 30

PAGE 56

1. 44
2. 55
3. 82
4. 53
5. 43
6. 13
7. 26
8. 24
9. 27
10. 66
11. 22
12. 22
13. 3
14. 73
15. 25
16. 33
17. 70
18. 26
19. 13
20. 72

PAGE 57

1. 65
2. 42
3. 41
4. 60
5. 62
6. 15
7. 33
8. 37
9. 22
10. 36
11. 52
12. 24
13. 23
14. 63
15. 21
16. 38
17. 10
18. 72
19. 50
20. 64

MATH FACTS FOR
MINECRAFTERS

Multiplication & Division

grades 3-4

CONTENTS

MATH FACTS PROGRESS TRACKER

Date	Page Number or Skill Practiced	Number Correct in One Minute

MULTIPLICATION MATH FACTS WITH 2

1. $\begin{array}{r} 1 \\ \times 2 \\ \hline \end{array}$
2. $\begin{array}{r} 2 \\ \times 2 \\ \hline \end{array}$
3. $\begin{array}{r} 3 \\ \times 2 \\ \hline \end{array}$
4. $\begin{array}{r} 4 \\ \times 2 \\ \hline \end{array}$
5. $\begin{array}{r} 5 \\ \times 2 \\ \hline \end{array}$

6. $\begin{array}{r} 6 \\ \times 2 \\ \hline \end{array}$
7. $\begin{array}{r} 7 \\ \times 2 \\ \hline \end{array}$
8. $\begin{array}{r} 8 \\ \times 2 \\ \hline \end{array}$
9. $\begin{array}{r} 9 \\ \times 2 \\ \hline \end{array}$
10. $\begin{array}{r} 10 \\ \times 2 \\ \hline \end{array}$

11. $\begin{array}{r} 2 \\ \times 1 \\ \hline \end{array}$
12. $\begin{array}{r} 2 \\ \times 5 \\ \hline \end{array}$
13. $\begin{array}{r} 2 \\ \times 3 \\ \hline \end{array}$
14. $\begin{array}{r} 2 \\ \times 6 \\ \hline \end{array}$
15. $\begin{array}{r} 2 \\ \times 8 \\ \hline \end{array}$

16. $\begin{array}{r} 2 \\ \times 4 \\ \hline \end{array}$
17. $\begin{array}{r} 2 \\ \times 0 \\ \hline \end{array}$
18. $\begin{array}{r} 2 \\ \times 7 \\ \hline \end{array}$
19. $\begin{array}{r} 2 \\ \times 10 \\ \hline \end{array}$
20. $\begin{array}{r} 2 \\ \times 9 \\ \hline \end{array}$

MULTIPLICATION MATH FACTS WITH 2

1. 7
   x 2

2. 3
   x 2

3. 2
   x 2

4. 10
   x 2

5. 4
   x 2

6. 6
   x 2

7. 1
   x 2

8. 9
   x 2

9. 8
   x 2

10. 5
    x 2

11. 2
    x 3

12. 2
    x 7

13. 2
    x 1

14. 2
    x 10

15. 2
    x 8

16. 2
    x 4

17. 2
    x 0

18. 2
    x 5

19. 2
    x 9

20. 2
    x 6

DIVISION MATH FACTS WITH 2

1. 10
    ÷ 2

2. 2
    ÷ 2

3. 4
    ÷ 2

4. 8
    ÷ 2

5. 6
    ÷ 2

6. 2
    ÷ 1

7. 0
    ÷ 2

8. 12
    ÷ 2

9. 20
    ÷ 2

10. 40
    ÷ 2

11. 22
    ÷ 2

12. 18
    ÷ 2

13. 24
    ÷ 2

14. 80
    ÷ 2

15. 16
    ÷ 2

16. 14
    ÷ 2

17. 100
    ÷ 2

18. 60
    ÷ 2

19. 50
    ÷ 2

20. 26
    ÷ 2

DIVISION MATH FACTS WITH 2

1. 20 ÷ 2

2. 0 ÷ 2

3. 8 ÷ 2

4. 18 ÷ 2

5. 6 ÷ 2

6. 22 ÷ 2

7. 2 ÷ 1

8. 24 ÷ 2

9. 10 ÷ 2

10. 14 ÷ 2

11. 2 ÷ 2

12. 100 ÷ 2

13. 12 ÷ 2

14. 50 ÷ 2

15. 60 ÷ 2

16. 4 ÷ 2

17. 40 ÷ 2

18. 16 ÷ 2

19. 80 ÷ 2

20. 26 ÷ 2

MULTIPLICATION MATH FACTS WITH 5

1. 1
   x 5

2. 2
   x 5

3. 3
   x 5

4. 4
   x 5

5. 5
   x 5

6. 6
   x 5

7. 7
   x 5

8. 8
   x 5

9. 9
   x 5

10. 10
    x 5

11. 5
    x 1

12. 5
    x 6

13. 5
    x 3

14. 5
    x 2

15. 5
    x 8

16. 5
    x 4

17. 5
    x 0

18. 5
    x 7

19. 5
    x 10

20. 5
    x 9

MULTIPLICATION MATH FACTS WITH 5

1.   5
  x 9

2.   2
  x 5

3.   5
  x 1

4.   5
  x 6

5.   5
  x 3

6.   5
  x 7

7.   5
  x 8

8.   5
  x 4

9.   5
  x 0

10.   5
  x 2

11.   5
  x 10

12.   5
  x 5

13.   8
  x 5

14.   9
  x 5

15.   4
  x 5

16.   6
  x 5

17.   3
  x 5

18.   1
  x 5

19.   10
  x 5

20.   7
  x 5

DIVISION MATH FACTS WITH 5

1. 10
÷ 5

2. 30
÷ 5

3. 15
÷ 5

4. 5
÷ 5

5. 20
÷ 5

6. 5
÷ 1

7. 0
÷ 5

8. 25
÷ 5

9. 45
÷ 5

10. 30
÷ 5

11. 15
÷ 5

12. 20
÷ 5

13. 5
÷ 5

14. 40
÷ 5

15. 50
÷ 5

16. 55
÷ 5

17. 5
÷ 1

18. 35
÷ 5

19. 10
÷ 5

20. 60
÷ 5

DIVISION MATH FACTS WITH 5

1. 20
÷ 5

2. 30
÷ 5

3. 50
÷ 5

4. 55
÷ 5

5. 10
÷ 5

6. 0
÷ 5

7. 5
÷ 1

8. 100
÷ 5

9. 25
÷ 5

10. 60
÷ 5

11. 5
÷ 5

12. 20
÷ 5

13. 5
÷ 1

14. 40
÷ 5

15. 15
÷ 5

16. 35
÷ 5

17. 5
÷ 5

18. 45
÷ 5

19. 10
÷ 5

20. 30
÷ 5

MULTIPLICATION MATH FACTS WITH 10

1. 1
   x 10

2. 2
   x 10

3. 3
   x 10

4. 4
   x 10

5. 5
   x 10

6. 6
   x 10

7. 7
   x 10

8. 8
   x 10

9. 9
   x 10

10. 10
    x 10

11. 10
    x 1

12. 10
    x 6

13. 10
    x 3

14. 10
    x 2

15. 10
    x 8

16. 10
    x 4

17. 10
    x 0

18. 10
    x 7

19. 10
    x 10

20. 10
    x 9

MULTIPLICATION MATH FACTS WITH 10

1. $\begin{array}{r} 10 \\ \times\ 6 \\ \hline \end{array}$

2. $\begin{array}{r} 10 \\ \times\ 1 \\ \hline \end{array}$

3. $\begin{array}{r} 10 \\ \times\ 3 \\ \hline \end{array}$

4. $\begin{array}{r} 10 \\ \times\ 2 \\ \hline \end{array}$

5. $\begin{array}{r} 10 \\ \times\ 8 \\ \hline \end{array}$

6. $\begin{array}{r} 10 \\ \times\ 0 \\ \hline \end{array}$

7. $\begin{array}{r} 10 \\ \times\ 4 \\ \hline \end{array}$

8. $\begin{array}{r} 10 \\ \times\ 7 \\ \hline \end{array}$

9. $\begin{array}{r} 10 \\ \times 10 \\ \hline \end{array}$

10. $\begin{array}{r} 10 \\ \times\ 9 \\ \hline \end{array}$

11. $\begin{array}{r} 2 \\ \times 10 \\ \hline \end{array}$

12. $\begin{array}{r} 1 \\ \times 10 \\ \hline \end{array}$

13. $\begin{array}{r} 3 \\ \times 10 \\ \hline \end{array}$

14. $\begin{array}{r} 4 \\ \times 10 \\ \hline \end{array}$

15. $\begin{array}{r} 5 \\ \times 10 \\ \hline \end{array}$

16. $\begin{array}{r} 7 \\ \times 10 \\ \hline \end{array}$

17. $\begin{array}{r} 6 \\ \times 10 \\ \hline \end{array}$

18. $\begin{array}{r} 8 \\ \times 10 \\ \hline \end{array}$

19. $\begin{array}{r} 9 \\ \times 10 \\ \hline \end{array}$

20. $\begin{array}{r} 10 \\ \times 10 \\ \hline \end{array}$

DIVISION MATH FACTS WITH 10

1. $10 \div 10$

2. $10 \div 1$

3. $30 \div 10$

4. $80 \div 10$

5. $10 \div 5$

6. $50 \div 10$

7. $70 \div 10$

8. $40 \div 10$

9. $100 \div 10$

10. $20 \div 10$

11. $0 \div 10$

12. $90 \div 10$

13. $30 \div 10$

14. $60 \div 10$

15. $10 \div 2$

16. $80 \div 10$

17. $10 \div 1$

18. $50 \div 10$

19. $70 \div 10$

20. $200 \div 10$

DIVISION MATH FACTS WITH 10

1. 100
÷ 10

2. 10
÷ 2

3. 30
÷ 10

4. 80
÷ 10

5. 90
÷ 10

6. 50
÷ 10

7. 40
÷ 10

8. 70
÷ 10

9. 20
÷ 10

10. 60
÷ 10

11. 0
÷ 10

12. 10
÷ 10

13. 100
÷ 10

14. 90
÷ 10

15. 10
÷ 1

16. 80
÷ 10

17. 10
÷ 5

18. 200
÷ 10

19. 10
÷ 10

20. 50
÷ 10

MULTIPLICATION MATH FACTS WITH 0 AND 1

1. 7
    x 0

2. 10
    x 1

3. 2
    x 1

4. 9
    x 1

5. 7
    x 1

6. 6
    x 0

7. 3
    x 1

8. 1
    x 1

9. 4
    x 0

10. 10
     x 0

11. 8
     x 0

12. 0
     x 0

13. 2
     x 0

14. 6
     x 1

15. 8
     x 1

16. 9
     x 0

17. 1
     x 0

18. 3
     x 0

19. 5
     x 0

20. 4
     x 1

MULTIPLICATION MATH FACTS WITH 0 AND 1

1. $\begin{array}{r} 0 \\ \times\, 0 \\ \hline \end{array}$

2. $\begin{array}{r} 1 \\ \times\, 1 \\ \hline \end{array}$

3. $\begin{array}{r} 9 \\ \times\, 1 \\ \hline \end{array}$

4. $\begin{array}{r} 3 \\ \times\, 1 \\ \hline \end{array}$

5. $\begin{array}{r} 2 \\ \times\, 1 \\ \hline \end{array}$

6. $\begin{array}{r} 1 \\ \times\, 0 \\ \hline \end{array}$

7. $\begin{array}{r} 5 \\ \times\, 1 \\ \hline \end{array}$

8. $\begin{array}{r} 10 \\ \times\, 1 \\ \hline \end{array}$

9. $\begin{array}{r} 4 \\ \times\, 0 \\ \hline \end{array}$

10. $\begin{array}{r} 3 \\ \times\, 0 \\ \hline \end{array}$

11. $\begin{array}{r} 9 \\ \times\, 0 \\ \hline \end{array}$

12. $\begin{array}{r} 8 \\ \times\, 0 \\ \hline \end{array}$

13. $\begin{array}{r} 7 \\ \times\, 1 \\ \hline \end{array}$

14. $\begin{array}{r} 6 \\ \times\, 1 \\ \hline \end{array}$

15. $\begin{array}{r} 4 \\ \times\, 1 \\ \hline \end{array}$

16. $\begin{array}{r} 7 \\ \times\, 0 \\ \hline \end{array}$

17. $\begin{array}{r} 1 \\ \times\, 10 \\ \hline \end{array}$

18. $\begin{array}{r} 2 \\ \times\, 0 \\ \hline \end{array}$

19. $\begin{array}{r} 5 \\ \times\, 0 \\ \hline \end{array}$

20. $\begin{array}{r} 8 \\ \times\, 1 \\ \hline \end{array}$

DIVISION MATH FACTS WITH 0 AND 1

1. $0 \div 5$

2. $10 \div 1$

3. $0 \div 2$

4. $12 \div 1$

5. $0 \div 2$

6. $2 \div 1$

7. $0 \div 15$

8. $0 \div 4$

9. $4 \div 1$

10. $0 \div 6$

11. $1 \div 1$

12. $7 \div 1$

13. $0 \div 8$

14. $0 \div 1$

15. $0 \div 3$

16. $14 \div 1$

17. $0 \div 9$

18. $5 \div 1$

19. $20 \div 1$

20. $0 \div 10$

DIVISION MATH FACTS WITH 0 AND 1

1. 10 ÷ 1

2. 0 ÷ 1

3. 0 ÷ 2

4. 8 ÷ 1

5. 5 ÷ 1

6. 2 ÷ 1

7. 15 ÷ 1

8. 0 ÷ 3

9. 6 ÷ 1

10. 0 ÷ 10

11. 0 ÷ 2

12. 12 ÷ 1

13. 1 ÷ 1

14. 0 ÷ 5

15. 20 ÷ 1

16. 4 ÷ 1

17. 0 ÷ 9

18. 0 ÷ 5

19. 7 ÷ 1

20. 0 ÷ 4

MULTIPLICATION MATH FACTS WITH 3

1. 3
   x 2

2. 3
   x 4

3. 3
   x 10

4. 1
   x 3

5. 3
   x 3

6. 3
   x 7

7. 3
   x 9

8. 3
   x 1

9. 3
   x 8

10. 5
   x 3

11. 4
   x 3

12. 3
   x 6

13. 10
   x 3

14. 7
   x 3

15. 8
   x 3

16. 9
   x 3

17. 2
   x 3

18. 3
   x 3

19. 6
   x 3

20. 0
   x 3

MULTIPLICATION MATH FACTS WITH 3

1. 4
    x 3

2. 3
    x 6

3. 3
    x 1

4. 7
    x 3

5. 8
    x 3

6. 9
    x 3

7. 2
    x 3

8. 3
    x 3

9. 6
    x 3

10. 0
    x 3

11. 3
    x 2

12. 3
    x 4

13. 3
    x 5

14. 1
    x 3

15. 10
    x 3

16. 3
    x 7

17. 3
    x 9

18. 3
    x 1

19. 3
    x 8

20. 5
    x 3

DIVISION MATH FACTS WITH 3

1. 6
    ÷ 3

2. 15
    ÷ 3

3. 30
    ÷ 3

4. 3
    ÷ 1

5. 9
    ÷ 3

6. 15
    ÷ 3

7. 0
    ÷ 3

8. 24
    ÷ 3

9. 21
    ÷ 3

10. 18
    ÷ 3

11. 33
    ÷ 3

12. 36
    ÷ 3

13. 3
    ÷ 3

14. 27
    ÷ 3

15. 12
    ÷ 3

16. 60
    ÷ 3

17. 90
    ÷ 3

18. 15
    ÷ 3

19. 9
    ÷ 3

20. 24
    ÷ 3

DIVISION MATH FACTS WITH 3

1. 33 ÷ 3

2. 15 ÷ 3

3. 3 ÷ 3

4. 3 ÷ 1

5. 9 ÷ 3

6. 18 ÷ 3

7. 0 ÷ 3

8. 60 ÷ 3

9. 6 ÷ 3

10. 99 ÷ 3

11. 21 ÷ 3

12. 36 ÷ 3

13. 90 ÷ 3

14. 24 ÷ 3

15. 27 ÷ 3

16. 12 ÷ 3

17. 30 ÷ 3

18. 0 ÷ 3

19. 15 ÷ 3

20. 39 ÷ 3

MULTIPLICATION MATH FACTS WITH 4

1. 9
    x 4

2. 7
    x 4

3. 4
    x 4

4. 4
    x 3

5. 5
    x 4

6. 8
    x 4

7. 2
    x 4

8. 4
    x 6

9. 1
    x 4

10. 4
    x 0

11. 4
    x 2

12. 4
    x 1

13. 6
    x 4

14. 7
    x 4

15. 8
    x 4

16. 4
    x 10

17. 4
    x 9

18. 0
    x 4

19. 4
    x 8

20. 4
    x 4

MULTIPLICATION MATH FACTS WITH 4

1.   6
  × 4

2.   3
  × 4

3.   4
  × 4

4.   4
  × 2

5.   1
  × 4

6.   9
  × 4

7.   2
  × 4

8. 10
  × 4

9.   4
  × 6

10.   0
  × 4

11.   4
  × 7

12.   4
  × 9

13.   4
  × 1

14.   4
  × 8

15.   5
  × 4

16.   4
  × 4

17.   4
  × 6

18.   4
  × 3

19.   7
  × 4

20.   8
  × 4

DIVISION MATH FACTS WITH 4

1. 12
    ÷ 4

2. 8
    ÷ 4

3. 16
    ÷ 4

4. 48
    ÷ 4

5. 24
    ÷ 4

6. 20
    ÷ 4

7. 4
    ÷ 4

8. 40
    ÷ 4

9. 4
    ÷ 1

10. 44
     ÷ 4

11. 80
     ÷ 4

12. 36
     ÷ 4

13. 28
     ÷ 4

14. 0
     ÷ 4

15. 24
     ÷ 4

16. 32
     ÷ 4

17. 4
     ÷ 4

18. 12
     ÷ 4

19. 16
     ÷ 4

20. 60
     ÷ 4

DIVISION MATH FACTS WITH 4

1. 28 ÷ 4

2. 16 ÷ 4

3. 8 ÷ 4

4. 40 ÷ 4

5. 24 ÷ 4

6. 32 ÷ 4

7. 0 ÷ 4

8. 4 ÷ 4

9. 4 ÷ 1

10. 44 ÷ 4

11. 80 ÷ 4

12. 32 ÷ 4

13. 12 ÷ 4

14. 0 ÷ 4

15. 20 ÷ 4

16. 36 ÷ 4

17. 44 ÷ 4

18. 16 ÷ 4

19. 8 ÷ 4

20. 4 ÷ 4

MULTIPLICATION MATH FACTS WITH 6

1. 6
  x 2

2. 6
  x 4

3. 6
  x 6

4. 12
  x 6

5. 10
  x 6

6. 6
  x 7

7. 6
  x 9

8. 6
  x 1

9. 6
  x 8

10. 5
  x 6

11. 6
  x 6

12. 3
  x 6

13. 6
  x 0

14. 7
  x 6

15. 8
  x 6

16. 9
  x 6

17. 2
  x 6

18. 6
  x 3

19. 6
  x 11

20. 0
  x 6

MULTIPLICATION MATH FACTS WITH 6

1. 6
   x 6

2. 3
   x 6

3. 6
   x 1

4. 7
   x 6

5. 8
   x 6

6. 4
   x 6

7. 2
   x 6

8. 6
   x 3

9. 6
   x 12

10. 0
   x 6

11. 6
   x 2

12. 6
   x 5

13. 6
   x 11

14. 12
   x 6

15. 10
   x 6

16. 6
   x 9

17. 6
   x 7

18. 6
   x 10

19. 8
   x 6

20. 5
   x 6

DIVISION MATH FACTS WITH 6

1. 36
÷ 6

2. 42
÷ 6

3. 60
÷ 6

4. 6
÷ 1

5. 12
÷ 6

6. 18
÷ 6

7. 6
÷ 6

8. 54
÷ 6

9. 24
÷ 6

10. 72
÷ 6

11. 66
÷ 6

12. 30
÷ 6

13. 0
÷ 6

14. 48
÷ 6

15. 18
÷ 6

16. 60
÷ 6

17. 6
÷ 1

18. 42
÷ 6

19. 36
÷ 6

20. 54
÷ 6

DIVISION MATH FACTS WITH 6

1. 66 ÷ 6

2. 30 ÷ 6

3. 0 ÷ 6

4. 48 ÷ 6

5. 18 ÷ 6

6. 60 ÷ 6

7. 6 ÷ 1

8. 42 ÷ 6

9. 36 ÷ 6

10. 54 ÷ 6

11. 6 ÷ 2

12. 42 ÷ 6

13. 60 ÷ 6

14. 6 ÷ 3

15. 12 ÷ 6

16. 18 ÷ 6

17. 6 ÷ 6

18. 54 ÷ 6

19. 24 ÷ 6

20. 72 ÷ 6

MULTIPLICATION MATH FACTS WITH 7

1. 6
    x 7

2. 3
    x 7

3. 7
    x 1

4. 7
    x 5

5. 8
    x 7

6. 4
    x 7

7. 2
    x 7

8. 7
    x 3

9. 7
    x 12

10. 0
     x 7

11. 7
     x 2

12. 5
     x 7

13. 7
     x 11

14. 12
     x 7

15. 10
     x 7

16. 7
     x 9

17. 7
     x 7

18. 7
     x 10

19. 7
     x 8

20. 11
     x 7

MULTIPLICATION MATH FACTS WITH 7

1. 7
   × 2

2. 7
   × 4

3. 7
   × 7

4. 12
   × 7

5. 10
   × 7

6. 7
   × 3

7. 7
   × 9

8. 7
   × 1

9. 7
   × 8

10. 5
    × 7

11. 4
    × 7

12. 3
    × 7

13. 7
    × 10

14. 7
    × 5

15. 8
    × 7

16. 9
    × 7

17. 2
    × 7

18. 7
    × 3

19. 7
    × 11

20. 0
    × 7

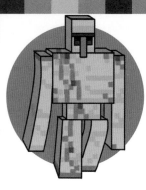

DIVISION MATH FACTS WITH 7

1. 49 ÷ 7

2. 42 ÷ 7

3. 14 ÷ 7

4. 28 ÷ 7

5. 35 ÷ 7

6. 70 ÷ 7

7. 56 ÷ 7

8. 7 ÷ 1

9. 63 ÷ 7

10. 77 ÷ 7

11. 7 ÷ 7

12. 21 ÷ 7

13. 0 ÷ 7

14. 49 ÷ 7

15. 84 ÷ 7

16. 14 ÷ 7

17. 42 ÷ 7

18. 35 ÷ 7

19. 7 ÷ 1

20. 70 ÷ 7

DIVISION MATH FACTS WITH 7

1. 42
÷ 7

2. 63
÷ 7

3. 70
÷ 7

4. 49
÷ 7

5. 77
÷ 7

6. 14
÷ 7

7. 56
÷ 7

8. 7
÷ 1

9. 28
÷ 7

10. 35
÷ 7

11. 7
÷ 7

12. 21
÷ 7

13. 7
÷ 7

14. 70
÷ 7

15. 42
÷ 7

16. 0
÷ 7

17. 84
÷ 7

18. 49
÷ 7

19. 7
÷ 1

20. 70
÷ 7

MULTIPLICATION MATH FACTS WITH 8

1. 8
    x 2

2. 8
    x 4

3. 8
    x 8

4. 12
    x 8

5. 10
    x 8

6. 8
    x 3

7. 8
    x 9

8. 8
    x 1

9. 8
    x 0

10. 5
     x 8

11. 4
     x 8

12. 3
     x 8

13. 8
     x 10

14. 8
     x 5

15. 8
     x 8

16. 9
     x 8

17. 2
     x 8

18. 8
     x 3

19. 8
     x 11

20. 0
     x 8

MULTIPLICATION MATH FACTS WITH 8

1.   6
  x 8

2.   3
  x 8

3.   8
  x 1

4.   8
  x 11

5.   8
  x 8

6.   4
  x 8

7.   2
  x 8

8.   8
  x 3

9.   8
  x 12

10.   0
  x 8

11.   8
  x 2

12.   5
  x 8

13.   8
  x 11

14. 12
  x 8

15. 10
  x 8

16.   8
  x 9

17.   8
  x 8

18.   8
  x 10

19.   8
  x 1

20.   5
  x 8

DIVISION MATH FACTS WITH 8

1. 16
    ÷ 8

2. 64
    ÷ 8

3. 32
    ÷ 8

4. 8
    ÷ 1

5. 56
    ÷ 8

6. 72
    ÷ 8

7. 8
    ÷ 8

8. 24
    ÷ 8

9. 40
    ÷ 8

10. 48
     ÷ 8

11. 88
     ÷ 8

12. 80
     ÷ 8

13. 0
     ÷ 8

14. 32
     ÷ 8

15. 96
     ÷ 8

16. 8
     ÷ 4

17. 16
     ÷ 8

18. 56
     ÷ 8

19. 8
     ÷ 2

20. 0
     ÷ 8

DIVISION MATH FACTS WITH 8

1. 88
  ÷ 8

2. 80
  ÷ 8

3. 0
  ÷ 8

4. 32
  ÷ 8

5. 8
  ÷ 8

6. 8
  ÷ 2

7. 16
  ÷ 8

8. 56
  ÷ 8

9. 8
  ÷ 4

10. 0
  ÷ 8

11. 24
  ÷ 8

12. 96
  ÷ 8

13. 64
  ÷ 8

14. 40
  ÷ 8

15. 48
  ÷ 8

16. 8
  ÷ 8

17. 64
  ÷ 8

18. 32
  ÷ 8

19. 8
  ÷ 1

20. 56
  ÷ 8

MULTIPLICATION MATH FACTS WITH 9

1.   6
   × 9

2.   3
   × 9

3.   9
   × 1

4.   9
   × 11

5.   9
   × 9

6.   4
   × 9

7.   2
   × 9

8.   9
   × 3

9.   9
   × 12

10.   0
   × 9

11.   9
   × 2

12.   5
   × 9

13.   9
   × 11

14.   12
   × 9

15.   10
   × 9

16.   9
   × 9

17.   1
   × 9

18.   9
   × 10

19.   9
   × 4

20.   5
   × 9

MULTIPLICATION MATH FACTS WITH 9

1. 9
    × 2

2. 9
    × 4

3. 9
    × 9

4. 12
    × 9

5. 10
    × 9

6. 9
    × 3

7. 8
    × 9

8. 9
    × 1

9. 9
    × 0

10. 5
     × 9

11. 4
     × 9

12. 3
     × 9

13. 9
     × 10

14. 9
     × 5

15. 9
     × 9

16. 9
     × 8

17. 2
     × 9

18. 9
     × 3

19. 9
     × 11

20. 0
     × 9

DIVISION MATH FACTS WITH 9

1. 90
    ÷ 9

2. 27
    ÷ 9

3. 81
    ÷ 9

4. 99
    ÷ 9

5. 72
    ÷ 9

6. 9
    ÷ 9

7. 36
    ÷ 9

8. 54
    ÷ 9

9. 45
    ÷ 9

10. 9
     ÷ 1

11. 0
     ÷ 9

12. 18
     ÷ 9

13. 108
    ÷ 9

14. 63
     ÷ 9

15. 27
     ÷ 9

16. 72
     ÷ 9

17. 54
     ÷ 9

18. 0
     ÷ 9

19. 9
     ÷ 1

20. 45
     ÷ 9

DIVISION MATH FACTS WITH 9

1. 99 ÷ 9

2. 18 ÷ 9

3. 108 ÷ 9

4. 63 ÷ 9

5. 27 ÷ 9

6. 81 ÷ 9

7. 54 ÷ 9

8. 0 ÷ 9

9. 9 ÷ 1

10. 45 ÷ 9

11. 9 ÷ 9

12. 27 ÷ 9

13. 72 ÷ 9

14. 0 ÷ 9

15. 90 ÷ 9

16. 18 ÷ 9

17. 36 ÷ 9

18. 54 ÷ 9

19. 45 ÷ 9

20. 9 ÷ 3

MATH FACTS REVIEW MULTIPLICATION

1. 4
    × 8

2. 9
    × 4

3. 2
    × 2

4. 6
    × 2

5. 7
    × 5

6. 5
    × 5

7. 3
    × 2

8. 2
    × 8

9. 9
    × 2

10. 3
     × 1

11. 8
     × 3

12. 8
     × 7

13. 6
     × 8

14. 9
     × 9

15. 7
     × 4

16. 3
     × 4

17. 4
     × 4

18. 6
     × 0

19. 10
     × 1

20. 5
     × 4

MATH FACTS REVIEW
MULTIPLICATION

1. 5
    × 2

2. 7
    × 7

3. 4
    × 2

4. 6
    × 4

5. 6
    × 6

6. 3
    × 6

7. 7
    × 2

8. 5
    × 4

9. 1
    × 9

10. 7
    × 9

11. 8
    × 9

12. 12
    × 3

13. 11
    × 2

14. 2
    × 2

15. 8
    × 8

16. 4
    × 7

17. 5
    × 5

18. 9
    × 3

19. 12
    × 2

20. 4
    × 4

MATH FACTS REVIEW
MULTIPLICATION

1. 5
    x 6

2. 7
    x 8

3. 9
    x 7

4. 6
    x 6

5. 1
    x 3

6. 5
    x 9

7. 8
    x 8

8. 3
    x 4

9. 10
    x 3

10. 9
     x 9

11. 5
     x 5

12. 3
     x 3

13. 9
     x 8

14. 7
     x 6

15. 6
     x 4

16. 7
     x 4

17. 9
     x 8

18. 8
     x 5

19. 2
     x 3

20. 4
     x 4

MATH FACTS REVIEW
MULTIPLICATION

1. 4
   x 9

2. 9
   x 5

3. 3
   x 2

4. 6
   x 3

5. 7
   x 6

6. 5
   x 6

7. 3
   x 3

8. 2
   x 9

9. 5
   x 2

10. 4
    x 1

11. 8
    x 0

12. 8
    x 7

13. 6
    x 4

14. 9
    x 9

15. 7
    x 5

16. 3
    x 3

17. 4
    x 5

18. 6
    x 1

19. 10
    x 2

20. 5
    x 8

MYSTERY NUMBER MULTIPLICATION MATH FACTS

Example:

1. 5
    × **6**
    ——
    30

2. ☐
    × 8
    ——
    56

3. 9
    × 7
    ——
    ☐

4. 6
    × ☐
    ——
    36

5. 1
    × ☐
    ——
    3

6. ☐
    × 5
    ——
    45

7. 8
    × ☐
    ——
    64

8. 8
    × ☐
    ——
    24

9. ☐
    × 3
    ——
    9

10. ☐
    × 9
    ——
    81

11. 5
    × ☐
    ——
    25

12. ☐
    × 3
    ——
    9

13. 9
    × ☐
    ——
    72

14. ☐
    × 6
    ——
    42

15. 6
    × 4
    ——
    ☐

16. 7
    × ☐
    ——
    28

17. 9
    × ☐
    ——
    36

18. 8
    × 5
    ——
    ☐

19. ☐
    × 3
    ——
    6

20. 4
    × ☐
    ——
    16

MATH FACTS REVIEW
DIVISION

1. 36
   ÷ 9

2. 45
   ÷ 5

3. 16
   ÷ 2

4. 18
   ÷ 3

5. 42
   ÷ 7

6. 30
   ÷ 6

7. 81
   ÷ 9

8. 72
   ÷ 9

9. 15
   ÷ 3

10. 0
    ÷ 4

11. 12
    ÷ 1

12. 56
    ÷ 7

13. 24
    ÷ 4

14. 24
    ÷ 3

15. 35
    ÷ 7

16. 99
    ÷ 11

17. 20
    ÷ 4

18. 50
    ÷ 10

19. 48
    ÷ 8

20. 40
    ÷ 5

MATH FACTS
REVIEW DIVISION

1. 27
   ÷ 9

2. 40
   ÷ 5

3. 16
   ÷ 8

4. 18
   ÷ 6

5. 42
   ÷ 6

6. 36
   ÷ 6

7. 81
   ÷ 9

8. 72
   ÷ 9

9. 15
   ÷ 5

10. 0
    ÷ 6

11. 10
    ÷ 1

12. 49
    ÷ 7

13. 24
    ÷ 6

14. 24
    ÷ 3

15. 35
    ÷ 7

16. 9
    ÷ 3

17. 20
    ÷ 5

18. 70
    ÷ 10

19. 48
    ÷ 8

20. 45
    ÷ 5

MATH FACTS
REVIEW DIVISION

1. 10 ÷ 2

2. 42 ÷ 7

3. 24 ÷ 6

4. 24 ÷ 3

5. 35 ÷ 5

6. 9 ÷ 9

7. 20 ÷ 4

8. 70 ÷ 10

9. 40 ÷ 8

10. 45 ÷ 5

11. 54 ÷ 9

12. 55 ÷ 5

13. 16 ÷ 8

14. 18 ÷ 6

15. 48 ÷ 6

16. 30 ÷ 6

17. 32 ÷ 8

18. 72 ÷ 9

19. 25 ÷ 5

20. 36 ÷ 12

MATH FACTS
REVIEW DIVISION

1. 100 ÷ 10

2. 21 ÷ 7

3. 54 ÷ 6

4. 27 ÷ 3

5. 30 ÷ 5

6. 4 ÷ 4

7. 0 ÷ 1

8. 10 ÷ 10

9. 40 ÷ 4

10. 55 ÷ 5

11. 72 ÷ 9

12. 40 ÷ 5

13. 12 ÷ 3

14. 18 ÷ 3

15. 42 ÷ 6

16. 18 ÷ 6

17. 64 ÷ 8

18. 81 ÷ 9

19. 24 ÷ 2

20. 16 ÷ 4

MYSTERY NUMBER DIVISION MATH FACTS

1. 32 ÷ ☐ = 8

2. ☐ ÷ 5 = 9

3. 9 ÷ 3 = ☐

4. ☐ ÷ 3 = 6

5. 42 ÷ ☐ = 6

6. 30 ÷ 3 = ☐

7. 15 ÷ ☐ = 5

8. 18 ÷ ☐ = 9

9. 10 ÷ ☐ = 10

10. 40 ÷ ☐ = 4

11. 8 ÷ ☐ = 4

12. ☐ ÷ 7 = 8

13. ☐ ÷ 4 = 6

14. 9 ÷ 9 = ☐

15. ☐ ÷ 5 = 6

16. 81 ÷ 9 = ☐

17. ☐ ÷ 5 = 2

18. 36 ÷ ☐ = 6

19. 100 ÷ ☐ = 10

20. ☐ ÷ 8 = 5

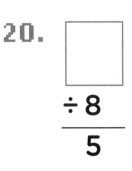

ANSWERS

PAGE 70

1. 2
2. 4
3. 6
4. 8
5. 10
6. 12
7. 14
8. 16
9. 18
10. 20
11. 2
12. 10
13. 6
14. 12
15. 16
16. 8
17. 0
18. 14
19. 20
20. 18

PAGE 71

1. 14
2. 6
3. 4
4. 20
5. 8
6. 12
7. 2
8. 18
9. 16
10. 10
11. 6
12. 14
13. 2
14. 20
15. 16
16. 8
17. 0
18. 10
19. 18
20. 12

PAGE 72

1. 5
2. 1
3. 2
4. 4
5. 3
6. 2
7. 0
8. 6
9. 10
10. 20
11. 11
12. 9
13. 12
14. 40
15. 8
16. 7
17. 50
18. 30
19. 25
20. 13

PAGE 73

1. 10
2. 0
3. 4
4. 9
5. 3
6. 11
7. 2
8. 12
9. 5
10. 7
11. 1
12. 50
13. 6
14. 25
15. 30
16. 2
17. 20
18. 8
19. 40
20. 13

PAGE 74

1. 5
2. 10
3. 15
4. 20
5. 25
6. 30
7. 35
8. 40
9. 45
10. 50
11. 5
12. 30
13. 15
14. 10
15. 40
16. 20
17. 0
18. 35
19. 50
20. 45

PAGE 75

1. 45
2. 10
3. 5
4. 30
5. 15
6. 35
7. 40
8. 20
9. 0
10. 10
11. 50
12. 25
13. 40
14. 45
15. 20
16. 30
17. 15
18. 5
19. 50
20. 35

PAGE 76

1. 2
2. 6
3. 3
4. 1
5. 4
6. 5
7. 0
8. 5
9. 9
10. 6
11. 3
12. 4
13. 1
14. 8
15. 10
16. 11
17. 5
18. 7
19. 2
20. 12

PAGE 77

1. 4
2. 6
3. 10
4. 11
5. 2
6. 0
7. 5
8. 20
9. 5
10. 12
11. 1
12. 4
13. 5
14. 8
15. 3
16. 7
17. 1
18. 9
19. 2
20. 6

PAGE 78

1. 10
2. 20
3. 30
4. 40
5. 50
6. 60
7. 70
8. 80
9. 90
10. 100
11. 10
12. 60
13. 30
14. 20
15. 80
16. 40
17. 0
18. 70
19. 100
20. 90

PAGE 79

1. 60
2. 10
3. 30
4. 20
5. 80
6. 0
7. 40
8. 70
9. 100
10. 90
11. 20
12. 10
13. 30
14. 40
15. 50
16. 70
17. 60
18. 80
19. 90
20. 100

PAGE 80

1. 1
2. 10
3. 3
4. 8
5. 2
6. 5
7. 7
8. 4
9. 10
10. 2
11. 0
12. 9
13. 3
14. 6
15. 5
16. 8
17. 10
18. 5
19. 7
20. 20

PAGE 81

1. 10
2. 5
3. 3
4. 8
5. 9
6. 5
7. 4
8. 7
9. 2
10. 6
11. 0
12. 1
13. 10
14. 9
15. 10
16. 8
17. 2
18. 20
19. 1
20. 5

PAGE 82

1. 0
2. 10
3. 2
4. 9
5. 7
6. 0
7. 3
8. 1
9. 0
10. 0
11. 0
12. 0
13. 0
14. 6
15. 8
16. 0
17. 0
18. 0
19. 0
20. 4

PAGE 83

1. 0
2. 1
3. 9
4. 3
5. 2
6. 0
7. 5
8. 10
9. 0
10. 0
11. 0
12. 0
13. 7
14. 6
15. 4
16. 0
17. 10
18. 0
19. 0
20. 8

PAGE 84

1. 0
2. 10
3. 0
4. 12
5. 0
6. 2
7. 0
8. 0
9. 4
10. 0
11. 1
12. 7
13. 0
14. 0
15. 0
16. 14
17. 0
18. 5
19. 20
20. 0

PAGE 85

1. 10
2. 0
3. 0
4. 8
5. 5
6. 2
7. 15
8. 0
9. 6
10. 0
11. 0
12. 12
13. 1
14. 0
15. 20
16. 4
17. 0
18. 0
19. 7
20. 0

PAGE 86

1. 6
2. 12
3. 30
4. 3
5. 9
6. 21
7. 27
8. 3
9. 24
10. 15
11. 12
12. 18
13. 30
14. 21
15. 24
16. 27
17. 6
18. 9
19. 18
20. 0

PAGE 87

1. 12
2. 18
3. 3
4. 21
5. 24
6. 27
7. 6
8. 9
9. 18
10. 0
11. 6
12. 12
13. 15
14. 3
15. 30
16. 21
17. 27
18. 3
19. 24
20. 15

PAGE 88

1. 2
2. 5
3. 10
4. 3
5. 3
6. 5
7. 0
8. 8
9. 7
10. 6
11. 11
12. 12
13. 1
14. 9
15. 4
16. 20
17. 30
18. 5
19. 3
20. 8

PAGE 89

1. 11
2. 5
3. 1
4. 3
5. 3
6. 6
7. 0
8. 20
9. 2
10. 33
11. 7
12. 12
13. 30
14. 8
15. 9
16. 4
17. 10
18. 0
19. 5
20. 13

PAGE 90

1. 36
2. 28
3. 16
4. 12
5. 20
6. 32
7. 8
8. 24
9. 4
10. 0
11. 8
12. 4
13. 24
14. 28
15. 32
16. 40
17. 36
18. 0
19. 32
20. 16

PAGE 91

1. 24
2. 12
3. 16
4. 8
5. 4
6. 36
7. 8
8. 40
9. 24
10. 0
11. 28
12. 36
13. 4
14. 32
15. 20
16. 16
17. 24
18. 12
19. 28
20. 32

PAGE 92

1. 3
2. 2
3. 4
4. 12
5. 6
6. 5
7. 1
8. 10
9. 4
10. 11
11. 20
12. 9
13. 7
14. 0
15. 6
16. 8
17. 1
18. 3
19. 4
20. 15

PAGE 93

1. 7
2. 4
3. 2
4. 10
5. 6
6. 8
7. 0
8. 1
9. 4
10. 11
11. 20
12. 8
13. 3
14. 0
15. 5
16. 9
17. 11
18. 4
19. 2
20. 1

PAGE 94

1. 12
2. 24
3. 36
4. 72
5. 60
6. 42
7. 54
8. 6
9. 48
10. 30
11. 36
12. 18
13. 0
14. 42
15. 48
16. 54
17. 12
18. 18
19. 66
20. 0

PAGE 95

1. 36
2. 18
3. 6
4. 42
5. 48
6. 24
7. 12
8. 18
9. 72
10. 0
11. 12
12. 30
13. 66
14. 72
15. 60
16. 54
17. 42
18. 60
19. 48
20. 30

PAGE 96

1. 6
2. 7
3. 10
4. 6
5. 2
6. 3
7. 1
8. 9
9. 4
10. 12
11. 11
12. 5
13. 0
14. 8
15. 3
16. 10
17. 6
18. 7
19. 6
20. 9

PAGE 97

1. 11
2. 5
3. 0
4. 8
5. 3
6. 10
7. 6
8. 7
9. 6
10. 9
11. 3
12. 7
13. 10
14. 2
15. 2
16. 3
17. 1
18. 9
19. 4
20. 12

PAGE 98

1. 42
2. 21
3. 7
4. 35
5. 56
6. 28
7. 14
8. 21
9. 84
10. 0
11. 14
12. 35
13. 77
14. 84
15. 70
16. 63
17. 49
18. 70
19. 56
20. 77

PAGE 99

1. 14
2. 28
3. 49
4. 84
5. 70
6. 21
7. 63
8. 7
9. 56
10. 35
11. 28
12. 21
13. 70
14. 35
15. 56
16. 63
17. 14
18. 21
19. 77
20. 0

PAGE 100

1. 7
2. 6
3. 2
4. 4
5. 5
6. 10
7. 8
8. 7
9. 9
10. 11
11. 1
12. 3
13. 0
14. 7
15. 12
16. 2
17. 6
18. 5
19. 7
20. 10

PAGE 101

1. 6
2. 9
3. 10
4. 7
5. 11
6. 2
7. 8
8. 7
9. 4
10. 5
11. 1
12. 3
13. 0
14. 10
15. 6
16. 0
17. 12
18. 7
19. 7
20. 10

PAGE 102

1. 16
2. 32
3. 64
4. 96
5. 80
6. 24
7. 72
8. 8
9. 0
10. 40
11. 32
12. 24
13. 80
14. 40
15. 64
16. 72
17. 16
18. 24
19. 88
20. 0

PAGE 103

1. 48
2. 24
3. 8
4. 88
5. 64
6. 32
7. 16
8. 24
9. 96
10. 0
11. 16
12. 40
13. 88
14. 96
15. 80
16. 72
17. 64
18. 80
19. 8
20. 40

PAGE 104

1. 2
2. 8
3. 4
4. 8
5. 7
6. 9
7. 1
8. 3
9. 5
10. 6
11. 11
12. 10
13. 0
14. 4
15. 12
16. 2
17. 2
18. 7
19. 4
20. 0

PAGE 105

1. 11
2. 10
3. 0
4. 4
5. 1
6. 4
7. 2
8. 7
9. 2
10. 0
11. 3
12. 12
13. 8
14. 5
15. 6
16. 1
17. 8
18. 4
19. 8
20. 7

PAGE 106

1. 54
2. 27
3. 9
4. 99
5. 81
6. 36
7. 18
8. 27
9. 108
10. 0
11. 18
12. 45
13. 99
14. 108
15. 90
16. 81
17. 9
18. 90
19. 36
20. 45

PAGE 107

1. 18
2. 36
3. 81
4. 108
5. 90
6. 27
7. 72
8. 9
9. 0
10. 45
11. 36
12. 27
13. 90
14. 45
15. 81
16. 72
17. 18
18. 27
19. 99
20. 0

PAGE 108

1. 10
2. 3
3. 9
4. 11
5. 8
6. 1
7. 4
8. 6
9. 5
10. 9
11. 0
12. 2
13. 12
14. 7
15. 3
16. 8
17. 6
18. 0
19. 9
20. 5

PAGE 109

1. 11
2. 2
3. 12
4. 7
5. 3
6. 9
7. 6
8. 0
9. 9
10. 5
11. 1
12. 3
13. 8
14. 0
15. 10
16. 2
17. 4
18. 6
19. 5
20. 3

PAGE 110

1. 32
2. 36
3. 4
4. 12
5. 35
6. 25
7. 6
8. 16
9. 18
10. 3
11. 24
12. 56
13. 48
14. 81
15. 28
16. 12
17. 16
18. 0
19. 10
20. 20

PAGE 111

1. 10
2. 49
3. 8
4. 24
5. 36
6. 18
7. 14
8. 20
9. 9
10. 63
11. 72
12. 36
13. 22
14. 4
15. 64
16. 28
17. 25
18. 27
19. 24
20. 16

PAGE 112

1. 30
2. 56
3. 63
4. 36
5. 3
6. 45
7. 64
8. 12
9. 30
10. 81
11. 25
12. 9
13. 72
14. 42
15. 24
16. 28
17. 72
18. 40
19. 6
20. 16

PAGE 113

1. 36
2. 45
3. 6
4. 18
5. 42
6. 30
7. 9
8. 18
9. 10
10. 4
11. 0
12. 56
13. 24
14. 81
15. 35
16. 9
17. 20
18. 6
19. 20
20. 40

PAGE 114

1. 6
2. 7
3. 63
4. 6
5. 3
6. 9
7. 8
8. 3
9. 3
10. 9
11. 5
12. 3
13. 8
14. 7
15. 24
16. 4
17. 4
18. 40
19. 2
20. 4

PAGE 115

1. 4
2. 9
3. 8
4. 6
5. 6
6. 5
7. 9
8. 8
9. 5
10. 0
11. 12
12. 8
13. 6
14. 8
15. 5
16. 9
17. 5
18. 5
19. 6
20. 8

PAGE 116

1. 3
2. 8
3. 2
4. 3
5. 7
6. 6
7. 9
8. 8
9. 3
10. 0
11. 10
12. 7
13. 4
14. 8
15. 7
16. 3
17. 4
18. 7
19. 6
20. 9

PAGE 117

1. 5
2. 6
3. 4
4. 8
5. 7
6. 1
7. 5
8. 7
9. 5
10. 9
11. 6
12. 11
13. 2
14. 3
15. 8
16. 5
17. 4
18. 8
19. 5
20. 3

PAGE 118

1. 10
2. 3
3. 9
4. 9
5. 6
6. 1
7. 0
8. 1
9. 10
10. 11
11. 8
12. 8
13. 4
14. 6
15. 7
16. 3
17. 8
18. 9
19. 12
20. 4

PAGE 119

1. 4
2. 45
3. 3
4. 18
5. 7
6. 10
7. 3
8. 2
9. 1
10. 10
11. 2
12. 56
13. 24
14. 1
15. 30
16. 9
17. 10
18. 6
19. 10
20. 40

MATH FOR MINECRAFTERS

Adventures in Addition & Subtraction

A NOTE TO PARENTS

When you want to reinforce classroom skills at home, it's crucial to have kid-friendly learning materials. This *Math for Minecrafters* workbook transforms math practice into an irresistible adventure complete with diamond swords, zombies, skeletons, and creepers. That means less arguing over homework and more fun overall.

Math for Minecrafters is also fully aligned with National Common Core Standards for 1st and 2nd grade math. What does that mean, exactly? All of the problems in this book correspond to what your child is expected to learn in school. This eliminates confusion and builds confidence for greater homework-time success!

As an added benefit to parents, the pages of this workbook are color coded to help you target specific skill areas as needed. Each color represents one of the four categories of Common Core math instruction. Use the chart below to guide you in understanding the different skills being taught at your child's school and to pinpoint areas where they may need extra practice.

BLUE	Operations and Algebraic Thinking
PINK	Numbers and Operations in Base 10
GREEN	Measurement and Data
ORANGE	Geometry

As the workbook progresses, the math problems become more advanced. Encourage your child to progress at his or her own pace. Learning is best when students are challenged, but not frustrated. What's most important is that your Minecrafter is engaged in his or her own learning.

Whether it's the joy of seeing their favorite game characters on every page or the thrill of solving challenging problems just like Steve and Alex, there is something in this workbook to entice even the most reluctant math student.

Happy adventuring!

ADDITION BY GROUPING

Circle Groups of 10. Then count and write the numbers.

Example:

1.

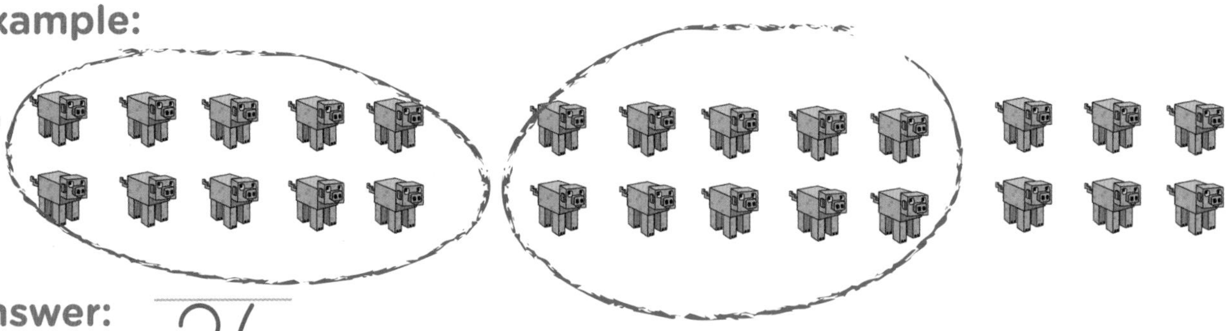

Answer: _26_

2.

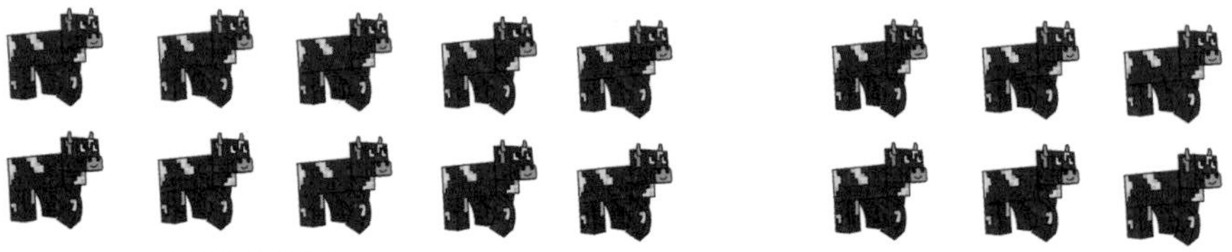

Answer: _____

3.

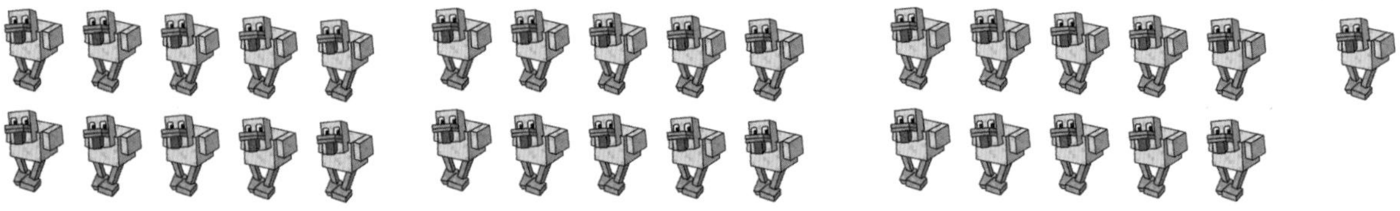

Answer: _____

4.

Answer: _____

5.

Answer: _____

MYSTERY MESSAGE
WITH ADDITION AND SUBTRACTION

Add or subtract. Then use the letters to fill in the blanks below and reveal the answer to Steve's joke.

1. 4 + 8 = 12 S

2. 6 - 3 = ___ N

3. 3 + 8 = ___ T

4. 7 - 5 = ___ M

5. 8 + 5 = ___ A

6. 8 - 2 = ___ R

7. 9 + 6 = ___ B

8. 10 - 3 = ___ L

9. 5 + 9 = ___ E

Q: Why do Minecraft horses eat golden apples and carrots with their mouths open?

A: Because they have bad...

COPY THE LETTERS FROM THE ANSWERS ABOVE TO SOLVE THE MYSTERY.

S ___ ___ ___ ___ ___
12 11 13 15 7 14

___ ___ ___ ___ ___ ___ S
2 13 3 3 14 6 12

ZOMBIE'S GUIDE TO PLACE VALUE

Use the number on each zombie to fill in the place-value chart. Then, write the number in tally marks.

Example: **1.**

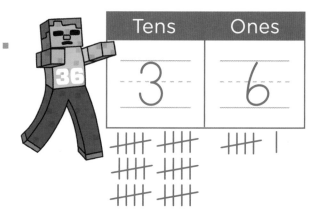

Tens	Ones
3	6

2.

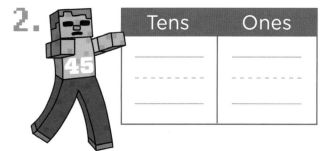

Tens	Ones

3.

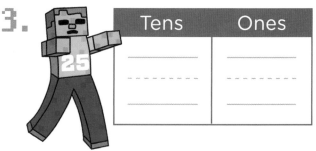

Tens	Ones

4.

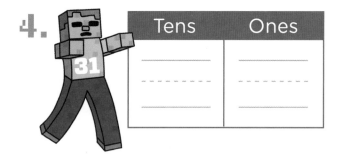

Tens	Ones

5.

Tens	Ones

6.

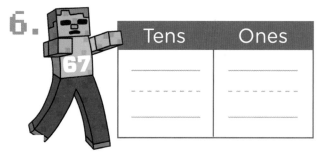

Tens	Ones

7.

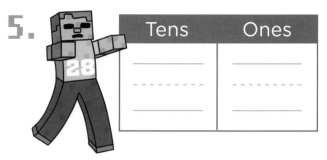

Tens	Ones

SKIP COUNT CHALLENGE

Count by 2s and fill in the empty spaces to keep Alex at a safe distance from the cave spider.

2   4   6   ___   ___   ___   ___   ___   ___   ___   ___   ___   26

TELLING TIME

Look at the clocks below and write the time in the space provided:

Example:

1.

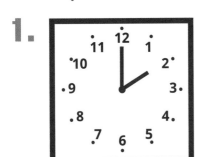

Answer:  2:00

2.

Answer: _____

3.

Answer: _____

4.

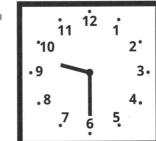

Answer: _____

5.

Answer: _____

6.

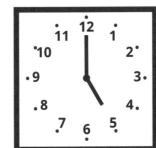

Answer: _____

COUNTING MONEY

*The villagers are letting you trade coins for emeralds.
Add up your coins to see how much money you have.*

25¢   10¢   5¢   1¢

1. 25¢ + 10¢ + 10¢ + 5¢ = 50¢

2. 10¢ + 5¢ + 5¢ + 1¢ + 1¢ + 1¢ = _____

3. 25¢ + 10¢ + 1¢ = _____

4. 25¢ + 25¢ + 5¢ + 5¢ = _____

5. 10¢ + 10¢ + 10¢ + 5¢ + 1¢ + 1¢ = _____

6. 25¢ + 5¢ + 5¢ + 5¢ + 1¢ = _____

7. 5¢ + 1¢ + 1¢ + 1¢ + 1¢ = _____

HARDCORE MODE: *Try this hardcore math challenge!*

8. One villager charges 25¢ for each emerald. How many (5¢) nickels do you need in order to buy the emerald?

_____

Answer: _____

ADVENTURES IN GEOMETRY

Let's learn about fractions! Count the number of squares in the crafting grid below.

Example: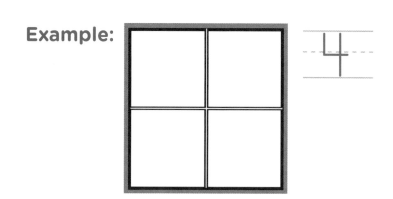

1. Color one of the four squares brown

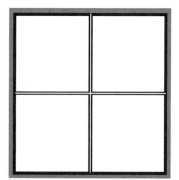

This is called one fourth, or ¼.

2. This crafting grid is divided into two equal parts. Color one of the two parts brown.

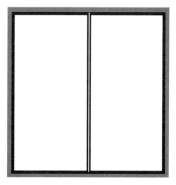

This is called one half, or ½.

3. Count the rectangles in the experience bar below.
Write the number here: _____

This experience bar is divided into 3 equal parts.
Color one part green.

This is called one third, or ⅓.

5. This experience bar is divided into 3 equal parts.
Color two parts green.

This is called two thirds, or ⅔.

HARDCORE MODE: *Try this hardcore math challenge!*
A health bar can show up to 10 hearts. Color in 5 hearts below.

Circle the fraction that describes how many are colored in:

A. 1/2   B. 1/4   C. 1/3

WORD PROBLEMS

Read the problem carefully. Use the picture to help you solve the problem. Fill in your answer.

Example:

You get 10 minutes of daylight in Minecraft. You lose 8 minutes building a shelter and finding food. How many minutes are left?

X	X	X	X	X	X	X	X		

$10 - 8 =$ 2

Answer: 2 minutes

1. You need 4 wooden planks to make a crafting table, but you only have 3. How many more planks do you need?

Answer: _____

2. There are 9 empty spaces in your inventory bar. You fill 4 spaces with tools. How many empty spaces do you have?

Answer: _____

3. 7 green experience orbs appear. You collect 3 of them. How many orbs are left to collect?

Answer: _____

4. You have 6 sheep on your farm. You add 2 pigs to the farm. How many animals do you have?

Answer: _____

5. You have 7 blocks of sandstone. You get 4 more blocks. How many blocks of sandstone do you have?

Answer: _____

6. 8 creepers are chasing you. 2 of them blow up! How many creepers are still chasing you?

Answer: _____

7. Alex has 7 potions in her inventory. She crafts 2 more potions. How many potions does she have?

Answer: _____

8. Yesterday you attacked 5 zombie pigmen. Today you attacked 8. How many more pigmen did you attack today than yesterday?

Answer: _____

GHAST'S GUIDE TO PLACE VALUE

Read the number on each ghast to fill in the place-value chart. Then, write the number in tally marks.

Example:

1.  **26**

Tens	Ones
2	6

‖‖‖ ‖‖‖   ‖‖‖ |
‖‖‖ ‖‖‖

2. **43**

Tens	Ones

3. **35**

Tens	Ones

4. **29**

Tens	Ones

5. **47**

Tens	Ones

6. **89**

Tens	Ones

7. **63**

Tens	Ones

SKIP COUNT CHALLENGE

Steve is tired after a long day of mining. Count by 5s and fill in the spaces to help him get home on his new railway system.

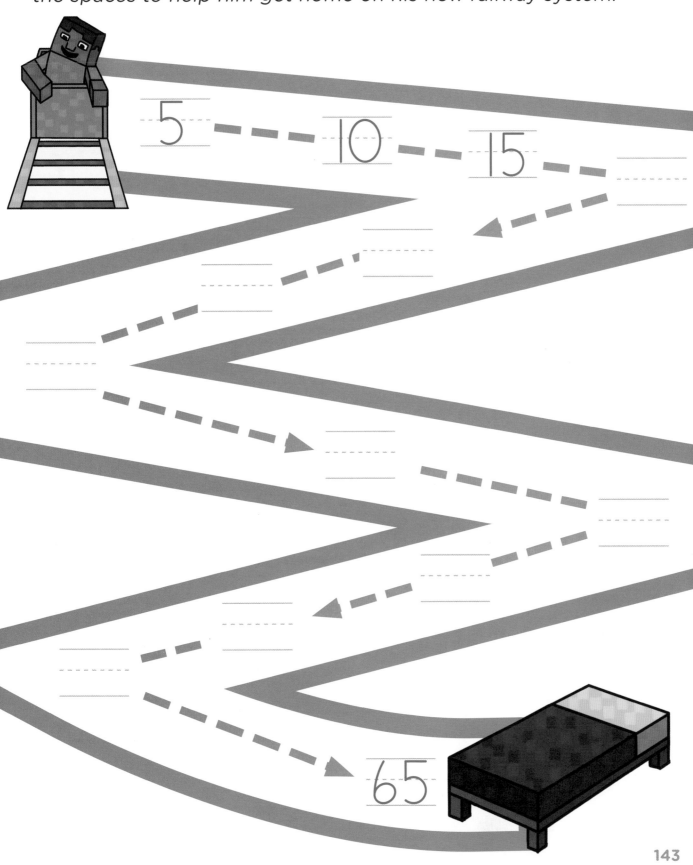

5 · · · 10 · · · 15

65

ALL IN A DAY'S WORK

A minecrafter's first day is very busy!
Match the time for each task on the left with a clock on the right.

1. 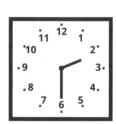 **6:00**
Smash a tree
to get wood.

2. 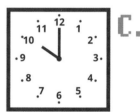 **7:30**
Make a pickaxe.

3. 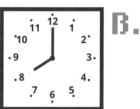 **9:00**
Get some wool.

4. 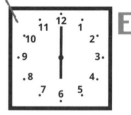 **10:00**
Build a bed.

5.  **2:30**
Build a shelter.

6. 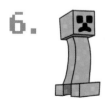 **8:00**
Hear a creeper
hiss nearby.

7.  **8:30**
Build a door
fast. Phew!

A.

B.

C.

D.

E.

F.

G.

TIME FOR MATCHING

Draw a big hand and a little hand on the clock to show the time.

Example:

3:00

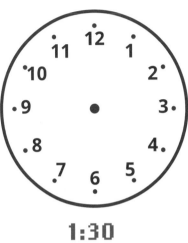

1:30

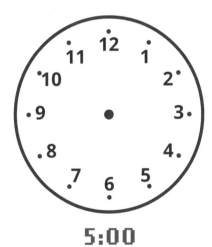

5:00

8:30

10:00

4:30

LEARNING ABOUT SHAPES

Draw along the dotted line to complete each shape. Connect the name of the shape to the correct drawing.

1. rectangle

A.

2. square

B.
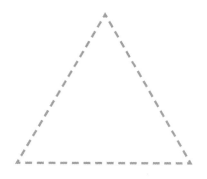

3. trapezoid

C.

4. triangle

D.
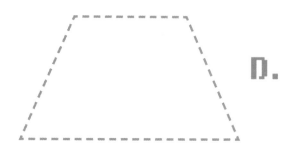

FIND THE SHAPES

Look at the items below and and use the word box to write the name:

square	circle	rectangle

5.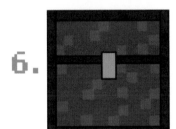

6.

7.

----

8. HARDCORE MODE: *Try this hardcore math challenge!*

Find 6 rectangles in this bottle of potion.

ADDITION BY GROUPING

Circle groups of 10 weapons and tools. Then count and write the total number.

Example:

1.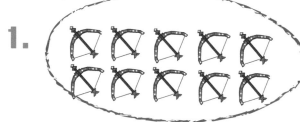

Answer:

2.

Answer: _____

3.

Answer: _____

4.

Answer: _____

5.

Answer: _____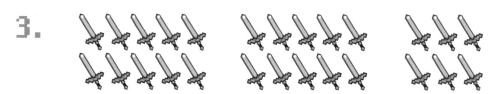

MYSTERY MESSAGE
WITH ADDITION AND SUBTRACTION

Add or subtract. Then use the letters to fill in the blanks below and reveal the answer to Steve's joke.

1. 12 + 8 = 20 H

2. 16 + 3 = ___ E

3. 11 – 8 = ___ A

4. 19 – 5 = ___ B

5. 14 + 3 = ___ Y

6. 16 + 2 = ___ N

7. 20 – 7 = ___ T

8. 18 – 3 = ___ D

9. 13 – 2 = ___ W

10. 17 - 9 = ___ O

11. 15 - 8 = ___ I

12. 12 + 4 = ___ G

Q: Why didn't the skeleton go to Alex's party?

COPY THE LETTERS FROM THE ANSWERS ABOVE TO FIND OUT.

H ___ H ___ ___ ___ ___
20 19 20 3 15 18 8

___ ___ ___ ___ ___ ___
14 8 15 17 13 8

___ ___ ___ ___ ___ H
16 8 11 7 13 20

149

THE ENDERMAN NUMBER CHALLENGE

Match the Enderman with the description of the number.

1.

Tens	Ones
8	4

2.

Tens	Ones
6	3

3.

Tens	Ones
5	9

4.

Tens	Ones
2	7

5.

Tens	Ones
7	2

A. 27

B. 59

C. 72

D. 84

E. 63

SKIP COUNT CHALLENGE

Count by 10s to help tame the ocelot. Feed it enough fish on this numbered path and you'll have a new pet!

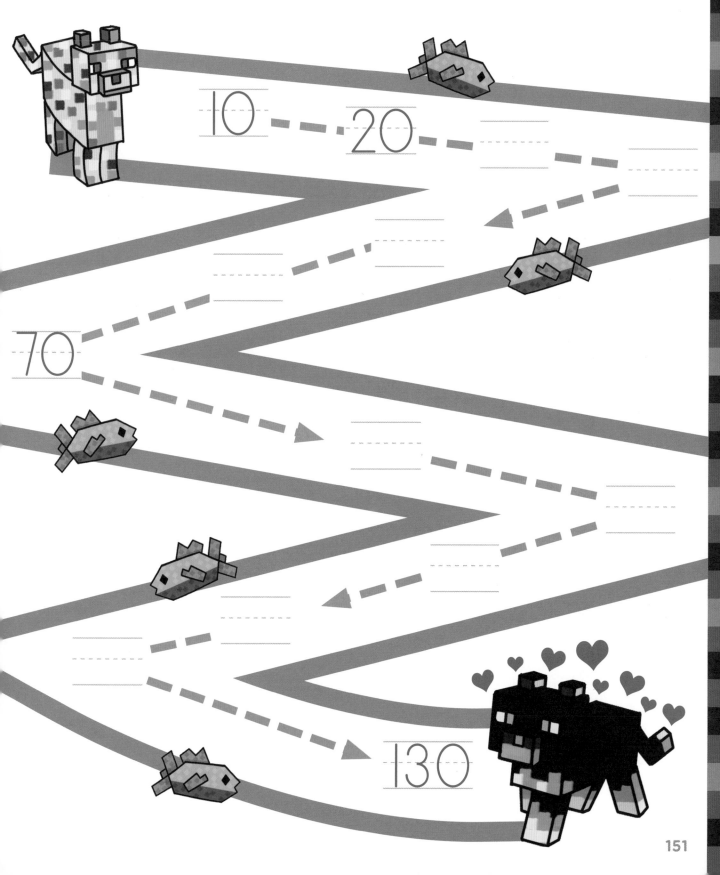

10 — 20

70

130

THE TALLEST TOWER

Steve built 3 watchtowers in different sizes to help him find his way home. Compare the towers and write your answers below.

How many blocks tall is each tower?

A.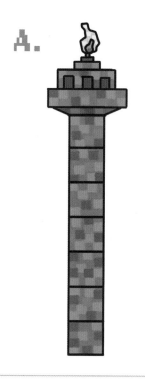

B.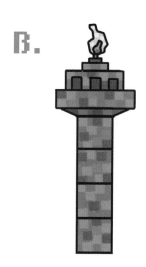

C.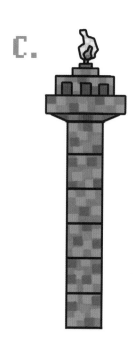

1. Which watchtower is the tallest?

2. Which watchtower is the shortest?

3. How much taller is watchtower A compared to watchtower B?

_____ **blocks.**

4. Draw your own watchtower, called watchtower D, in the space below. It must be taller than tower B, but shorter than tower C. Color it in using your favorite color!

D.

5. How many blocks tall is your watchtower? _____ **blocks.**

6. Fill in the rest of this table to keep track of all the different towers.

Tower	Number of Blocks Tall	Color
A	7	GRAY
B		
C		
D		

ADVENTURES IN GEOMETRY

Trace the dotted line to divide these shapes into 2 equal parts. Then color one half (½) of the shape.

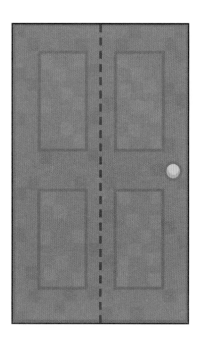

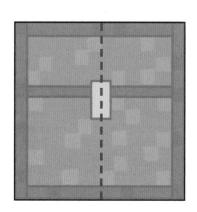

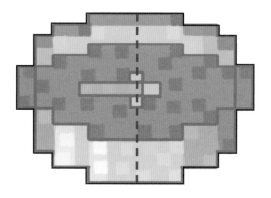

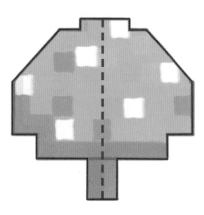

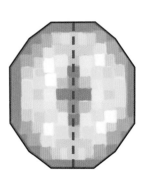

Trace the dotted line to divide these shapes into 4 equal parts. Then color in one quarter (¼) of each shape below.

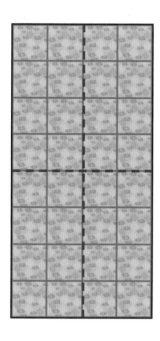

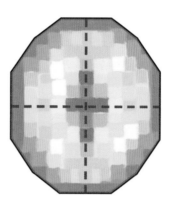

Color in one half of this wooden plank:

Color in one quarter of this wooden plank:

½

¼

WORD PROBLEMS

Read the problem carefully. Look at the picture and fill in your answer.

Example:

1. Steve eats 3 carrots. He attacks zombies, and they drop 2 more carrots and 2 potatoes for him to eat. How many food items does he eat all together?

$$3 + 2 + 2 = 7$$

Answer: 7

2. Alex gets 2 blocks of lava from a blacksmith's house, 5 more from the Nether, and 6 from an End Portal room. How many blocks of lava does she get in all?

Answer: _____

3. Steve sees 16 ghasts on his adventures. He destroys 4 with enchanted arrows and 3 more with fireballs. How many ghasts are left?

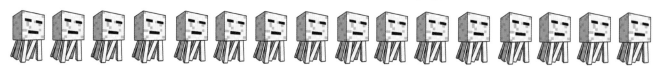

Answer: _____

4. In one day, Steve makes 10 pickaxes, 3 axes, and 9 shovels to attack mobs. How many weapons did he make in all?

Answer: _____

5. Alex gets 6 cookies from trading with a villager. She gets 7 more cookies later in the day and 4 more cookies in the morning. How many cookies does she have in all?

Answer: _____

6. You start your game with 20 hunger points. You lose 2 points running away from a creeper. You lose 4 more points attacking skeletons. How many hunger points are left?

Answer: _____

7. You start your game with 9 items in your inventory. You remove 4 tools and 2 food items. How many items are left in your inventory?

Answer: _____

8. Steve loves his pet cats. He has 4 in a fenced area outside, 7 in his house, and 5 in another fenced area. How many pet cats does he have?

Answer: _____

CREEPER'S GUIDE TO PLACE VALUE

Use the number on each creeper to fill in the place value chart.

Example:

1.  354

Hundreds	Tens	Ones
3	5	4

2. 760

Hundreds	Tens	Ones

3. 592

Hundreds	Tens	Ones

4. 184

Hundreds	Tens	Ones

5. 532

Hundreds	Tens	Ones

6. 956

Hundreds	Tens	Ones

7. 453

Hundreds	Tens	Ones

SKIP COUNT CHALLENGE

Fill in the blank spaces as you count from 110 to 125 and help Alex find her way back to her house.

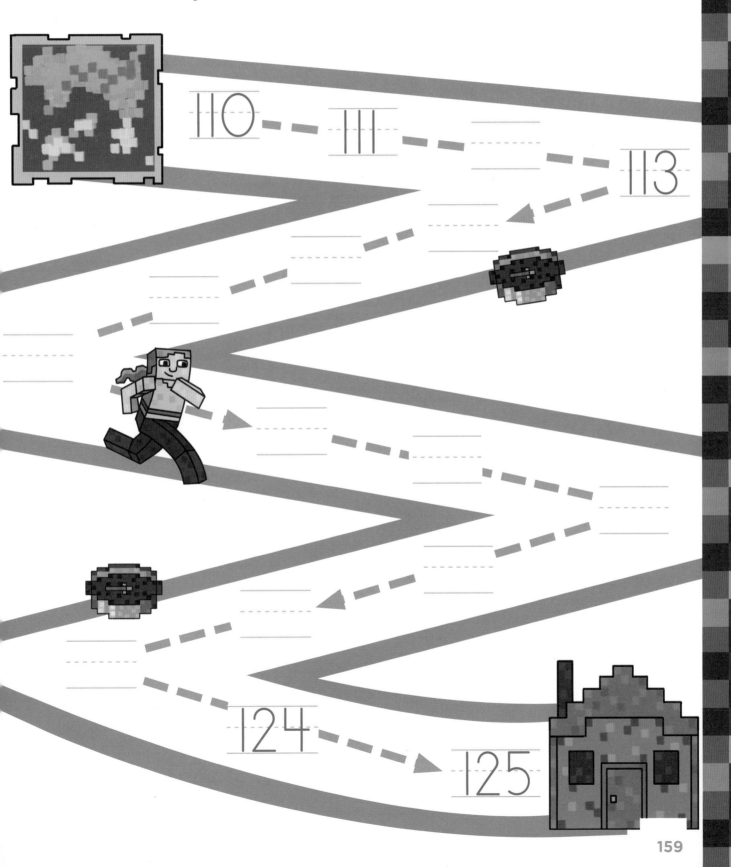

110 -- 111 -- 113

124 -- 125

MOBS AND MONSTERS

Video game characters are sometimes called Mobs. Add an X to the boxes that describe each mob in the table below.

	Creeper	Zombie	Ghast	Enderman	Cave Spider	Snow Golem
0 Legs						
2 Legs						
More than 2 Legs						

Use the table to answer these questions.

1. How many Mobs have more than 2 legs? _____

2. How many Mobs have 2 legs or less? _____

3. Which 2 Mobs are the same color, but have a different number of legs and eyes? _____

COUNTING MONEY

Steve wants to feed his farm animals the following items. Find out how much money each item costs and write the amount in the space provided.

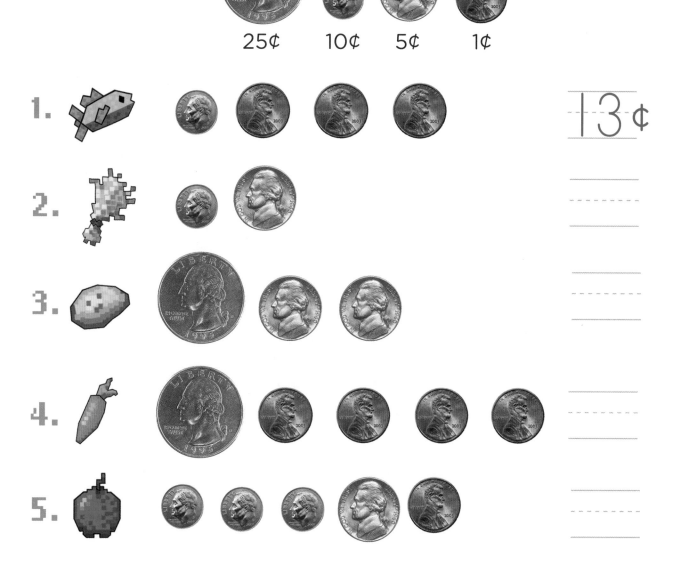

25¢   10¢   5¢   1¢

1.   13¢

2.

3.

4.

5.

HARDCORE MODE: *Try this hardcore math challenge!*

6. How much money does Steve need to buy all 7 of the food items listed above? Add them up to find out!

Answer: _____

ADVENTURES IN GEOMETRY: SPOT THE SHAPES

Look at the Minecrafter's house and answer the questions.
Use the shapes below to help you.

rectangle   square   trapezoid

1. What shape is the roof of this house?

2. What shape is the double window?

3. What shape is the doorknob?

CREATIVE MODE

Use a pencil or pen to change the roof into a triangle!

Draw your own Minecrafter's house in the space below. Use as many shapes as you can. Add fun details and color!

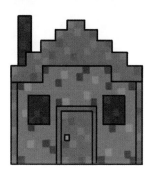

SANDSTONE ADDITION

Add the ones and then the tens to get the answer.

1. 50
    + 26
    _____

    D

2. 72
    + 25
    _____

    Q

3. 43
    + 32
    _____

    T

4. 20
    + 64
    _____

    E

5. 82
    + 15
    _____

    Z

6. 90
    + 8
    _____

    S

7. 83
    + 14
    _____

    M

8. 44
    + 30
    _____

    E

9. 25
    + 61
    _____

    R

10. 16
    + 43
    _____

    B

11. 24
    + 12
    _____

    T

12. 55
    + 54
    _____

    K

HIDDEN MESSAGE:

Even numbers end in 0, 2, 4, 6, or 8. Circle the EVEN numbered answers above. Write the letter from those blocks in order from left to right below to spell out the name of a biome with lots of sandstone:

_____ _____ _____ _____ _____ _____

SUBTRACTION MYSTERY MESSAGE

Subtract the ones, then the tens. Use the letters to fill in the blanks below and answer Steve's riddle.

1. 45
  − 32
  _____

  S

2. 89
  − 45
  _____

  C

3. 93
  − 32
  _____

  O

4. 27
  − 12
  _____

  I

5. 32
  − 11
  _____

  U

6. 94
  − 23
  _____

  E

7. 48
  − 37
  _____

  F

8. 74
  − 32
  _____

  R

9. 68
  − 42
  _____

  M

10. 86
  − 33
  _____

  P

Q: What music does a creeper enjoy most?
Copy the letters from the answers above to find out!

| 53 | 61 | 53 | | 26 | 21 | 13 | 15 | 44 |

| 61 | 11 | | 44 | 61 | 21 | 42 | 13 | 71 |

MOB MONSTER SHOWDOWN

Who has more attack power? Compare the number of times each Mob has attacked a player and write in the correct symbol.

> means greater than   **<** means less than

Example **1.** 385 392

2. 856   826

3. 445   454

4. 523   527

5. 672   607

6. 908   998

7. 746   772

Count up their wins and circle the one with the most wins below.

Skeleton   **Enderman**

SKIP COUNT CHALLENGE

Count by 3s to collect all of the ink from the squids.

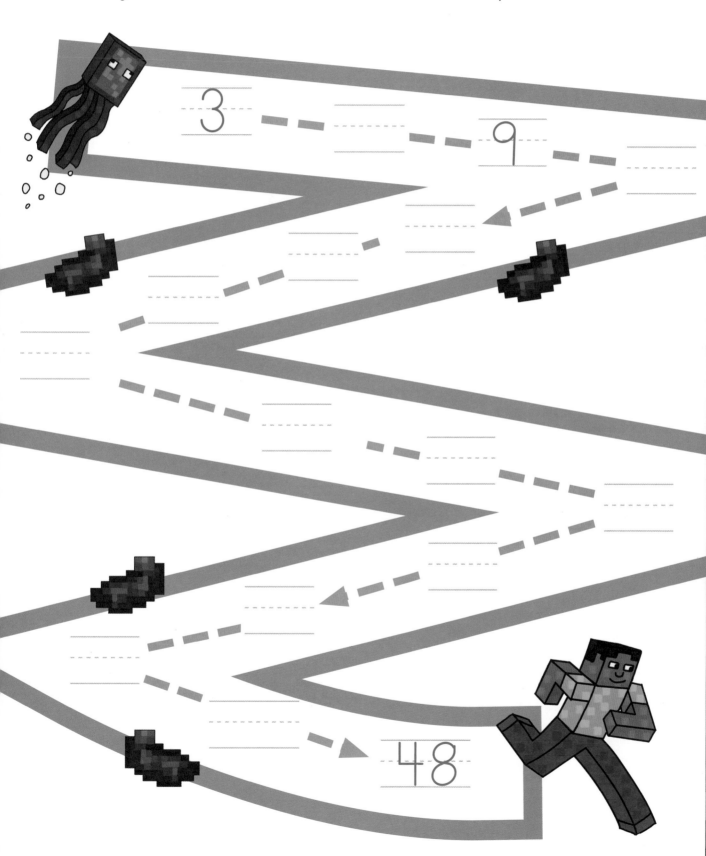

3 _____ 9 _____

48

TELLING TIME

Look at the clocks below and write the time in the space provided:

Example:

1.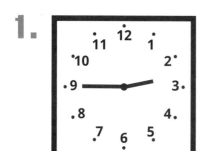

Answer: 2:45

2.

Answer: _____

3.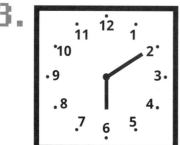

Answer: _____

4.

Answer: _____

5.

Answer: _____

6.

Answer: _____

7.

Answer: _____

8.

Answer: _____

9.

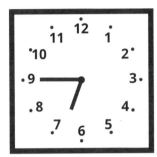

Answer: _____

10.

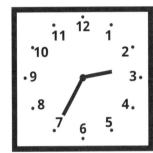

Answer: _____

11.

Answer: _____

12.

Answer: _____

13.

Answer: _____

14.

Answer: _____

4 SIDES ARE BETTER THAN 1

A Minecrafter's world is full of **quadrilaterals**. Find them and circle them below.

Hint: Quadrilaterals are closed shapes with 4 sides. Squares and rectangles are two kinds of quadrilaterals.

Can you find 3 purple quadrilaterals on this fish?

Can you find...
...9 quadrilaterals in this treasure chest?

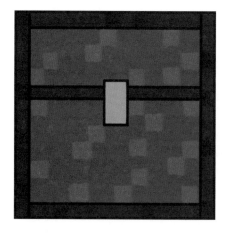

...7 quadrilaterals in this Minecrafter's house?

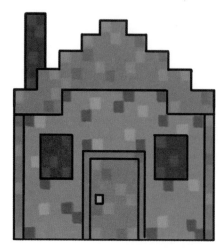

Trace the quadrilaterals below:

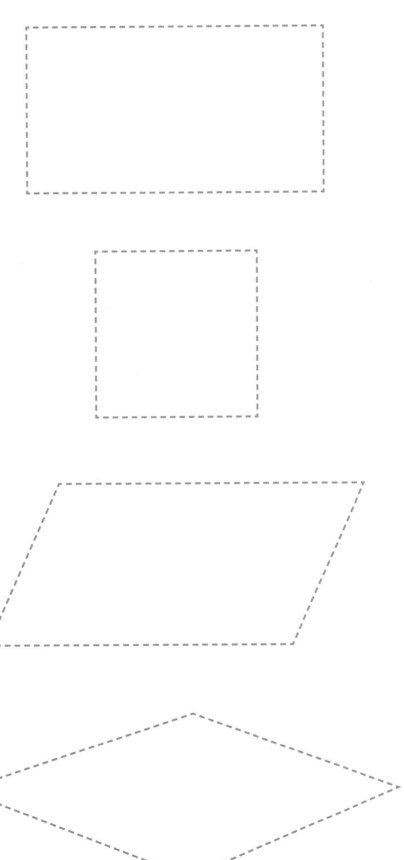

ADDITION & SUBTRACTION MYSTERY NUMBER

There is a number hidden behind these redstone blocks. Subtract or count on to find the mystery number.

1.
15
+
18

= 3

2.
22
+
29

=

3.
43
+
53

=

4.
17
+
25

=

5.
76
+
82

=

6.
50
+
64

=

7.
49
+
56

=

8.
27
+
30

=

9.
63
+
70

=

MYSTERY MESSAGE
WITH ADDITION USING REGROUPING

Add. Use the letters to fill in the blanks below and answer the riddle.

1. $\begin{array}{r} 45 \\ +\ 9 \\ \hline \end{array}$ 2. $\begin{array}{r} 89 \\ +\ 7 \\ \hline \end{array}$ 3. $\begin{array}{r} 33 \\ +\ 8 \\ \hline \end{array}$ 4. $\begin{array}{r} 27 \\ +13 \\ \hline \end{array}$ 5. $\begin{array}{r} 38 \\ +\ 6 \\ \hline \end{array}$

   O   T   N   E   I

6. $\begin{array}{r} 25 \\ +\ 6 \\ \hline \end{array}$ 7. $\begin{array}{r} 46 \\ +27 \\ \hline \end{array}$ 8. $\begin{array}{r} 74 \\ +19 \\ \hline \end{array}$ 9. $\begin{array}{r} 28 \\ +42 \\ \hline \end{array}$ 10. $\begin{array}{r} 56 \\ +16 \\ \hline \end{array}$

   F   R   H   S   A

Q: How many pieces of armor can you fit in an empty treasure chest?

___ ___ ___ . ___ ___ ___ ___ ___
54 41 40   72 31 96 40 73

___ ___ ___ ___ , ___ ___ ___
96 93 72 96   44 96 70

___ ___ ___ ___ M P ___ Y .
41 54 96 40   96

173

PIGMAN'S GUIDE TO PLACE VALUE

Identify the number that belongs in the place-value chart and write it there.

Example:

1.  534

Tens
3

2.  973

Hundreds

3.  462

Ones

4.  875

Hundreds

5.  546

Tens

6.  231

Ones

7.  952

Hundreds

SKIP COUNT CHALLENGE

Enter The End through The End portal and count by 4s until you reach the Enderdragon for an epic battle.

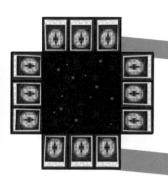

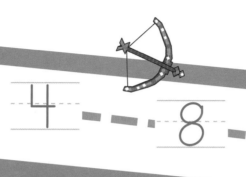

4   8   16

60

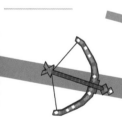

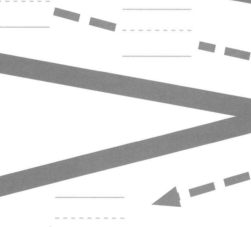

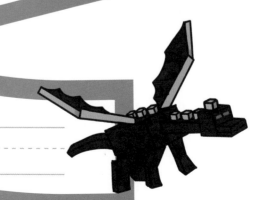

ANIMAL TALLY

Use the table to compare the animals that Alex and Steve have on their farms.

STEVE	|||	||	|||| ||	|||| |||| |||| ||
ALEX	||||	||||		||||		||||

1. How many sheep does Alex keep on her farm?

2. Who has more pigs, Steve or Alex?

3. Steve and Alex both have cows. How many *more* cows does Steve have?

4. If Steve and Alex put their chickens together on one farm, how many chickens would they have?

WEAPON TALLY

Use the table to compare the weapons that Steve and Alex have crafted.

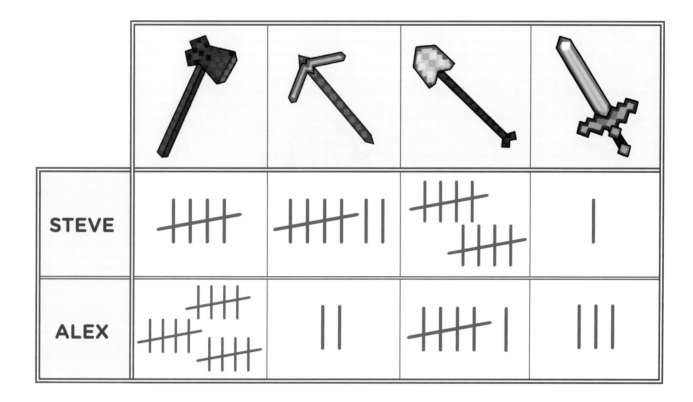

	Axe	Pickaxe	Shovel	Sword
STEVE	卌	卌卌 II	卌卌 卌	I
ALEX	卌 卌 卌	II	卌 I	III

1. How many shovels did Steve craft? - - - - - - - -

2. Steve and Alex both have diamond swords. How many *more* diamond swords does Alex have? - - - - - - - -

3. Steve and Alex both have axes. How many *more* axes does Alex have? - - - - - - - -

4. Who has the most pickaxes? -

ADVENTURES IN GEOMETRY: SPOT THE SHAPES

Can you spot: 14 **triangles** in this pile of gems?

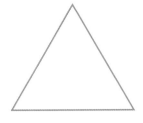

Can you spot: 6 **trapezoids** in this diamond armor?

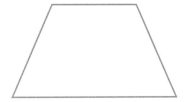

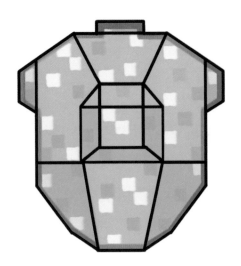

Use the words in the inventory bar to answer these questions.

octagon	quadrilateral	oval	sphere	cube

1. Which shape will this treasure chest be when it is closed?

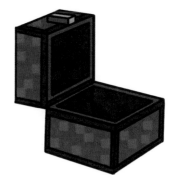

_____

2. Which shape always has 4 sides?

_____

3. Which shape is the face of this Minecraft clock?

_____

4. Which shape is a 3-D circle, like a round ball?

_____

5. What shape best describes this egg?

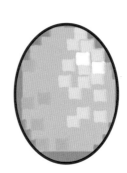

_____

WORD PROBLEMS

Write a number sentence to help you solve these word problems.

Example:

1. You break 13 dirt blocks with your diamond shovel. You also break 5 sand blocks and 3 gravel blocks. How many blocks do you break in all?

$$13 + 5 + 3 = 21$$

Answer: _21 blocks_

2. You get 17 mushrooms to make a stew. A cow eats 3 of them. You get 5 more mushrooms. How many mushrooms do you have now?

Answer: _____

3. You make 6 snow golems to protect your house. A zombie destroys 2 of them. You make 7 more. How many snow golems do you have now?

Answer: _____

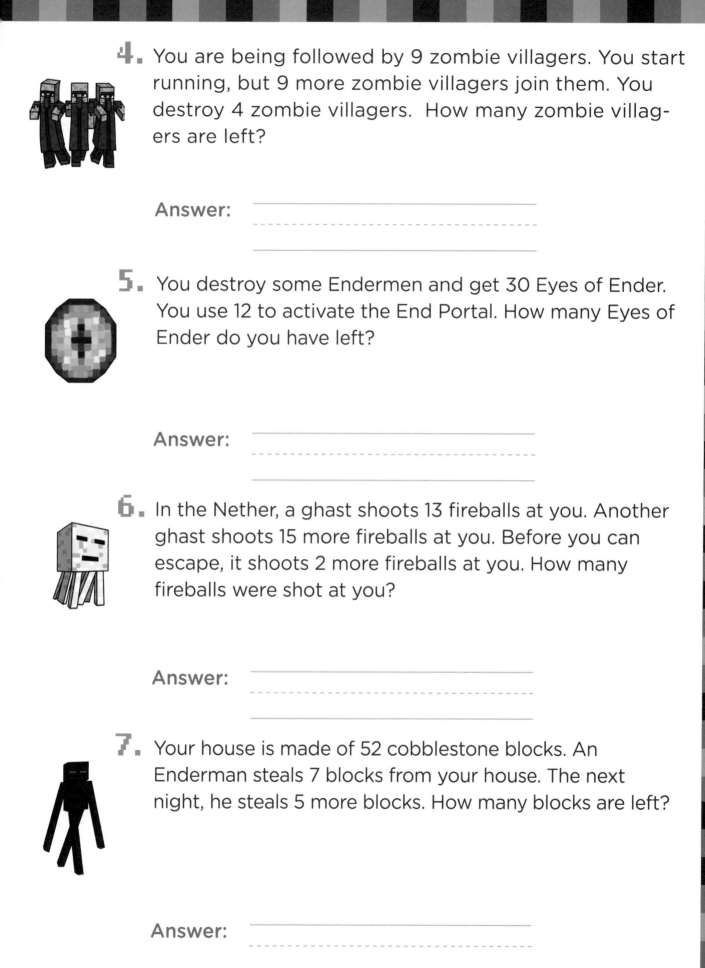

4. You are being followed by 9 zombie villagers. You start running, but 9 more zombie villagers join them. You destroy 4 zombie villagers. How many zombie villagers are left?

Answer: _____

5. You destroy some Endermen and get 30 Eyes of Ender. You use 12 to activate the End Portal. How many Eyes of Ender do you have left?

Answer: _____

6. In the Nether, a ghast shoots 13 fireballs at you. Another ghast shoots 15 more fireballs at you. Before you can escape, it shoots 2 more fireballs at you. How many fireballs were shot at you?

Answer: _____

7. Your house is made of 52 cobblestone blocks. An Enderman steals 7 blocks from your house. The next night, he steals 5 more blocks. How many blocks are left?

Answer: _____

IRON GOLEM'S GUIDE TO PLACE VALUE

Match the number on each Iron Golem to the place value descriptions on the right.

Example:

1.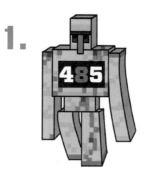

Tens
8

2.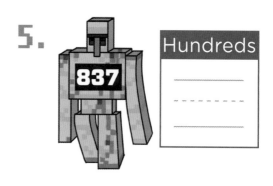

Ones

3.

Tens

4.

Ones

5.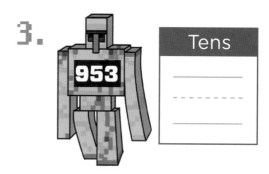

Hundreds

6.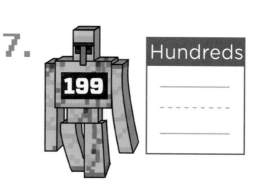

Tens

7.

Hundreds

SKIP COUNT CHALLENGE

Count by 100s to fill in the path and help tame this wolf with raw meat.

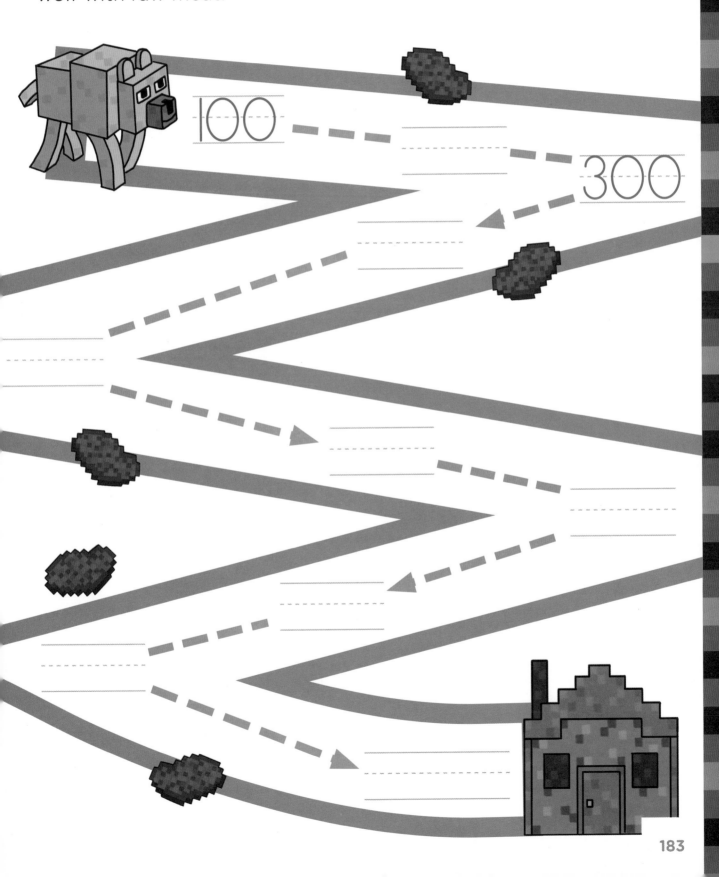

100

300

TELLING TIME

Look at the clocks below and write the time in the space provided:

1.

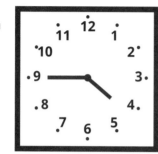

Answer: 4:45

2.

Answer: _____

3.

Answer: _____

4.

Answer: _____

5.

Answer: _____

6.

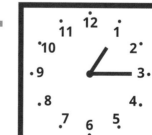

Answer: _____

COUNTING MONEY

How much money is hidden in each treasure chest? Add up the coins to find out.

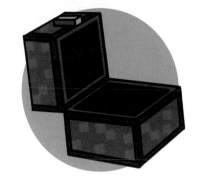

25¢   10¢   5¢   1¢

1. _____ 4 1 ¢

2. _____ - - - - - - - - -

3. _____ - - - - - - - - -

4. _____ - - - - - - - - -

5. _____ - - - - - - - - -

HARDCORE MODE: Try this hardcore math challenge!
Steve looks in a treasure chest and finds 4 coins that add up
to 40¢. There is only 1 kind of coin in the treasure chest.
What coin is it?   _____

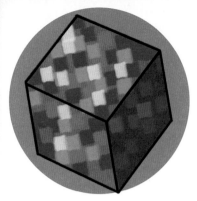

GEOMETRY

This wooden plank is divided into 4 equal parts called fourths. Color the wooden planks below according to the description.

1. Color: one fourth

¹/₄

2. Color: three fourths

³/₄

3. Color: two fourths

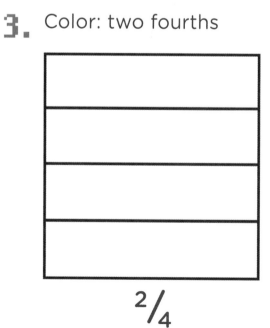

²/₄

4. Color: four fourths

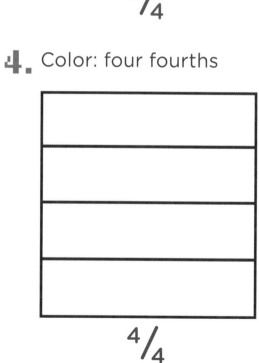

⁴/₄

5. Which set of planks above is the same as one half?

Match the shaded set of blocks to the correct fraction on the right.

6. 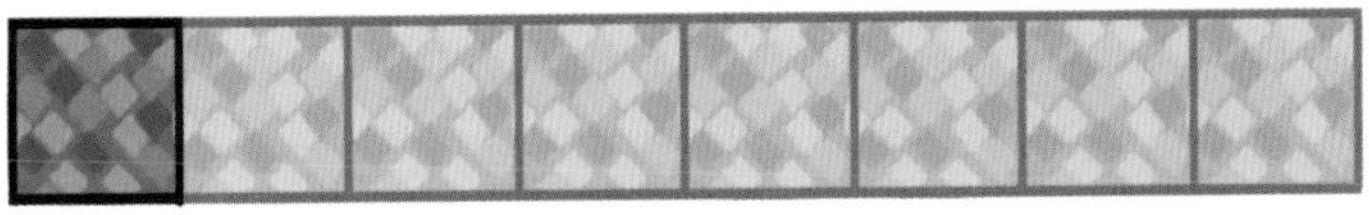 $\dfrac{5}{8}$

7. 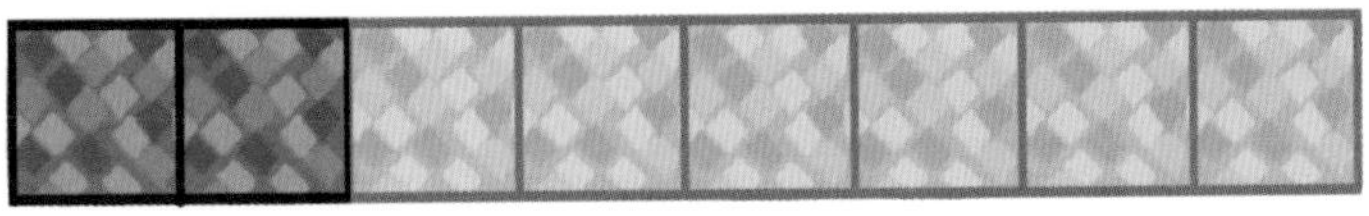 $\dfrac{3}{8}$

8. 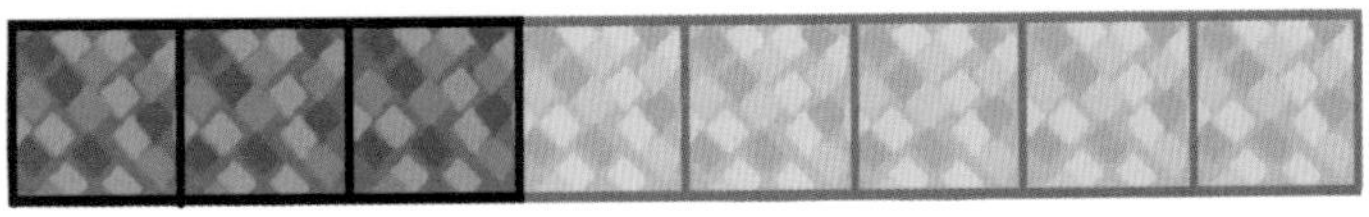 $\dfrac{2}{8}$

9. 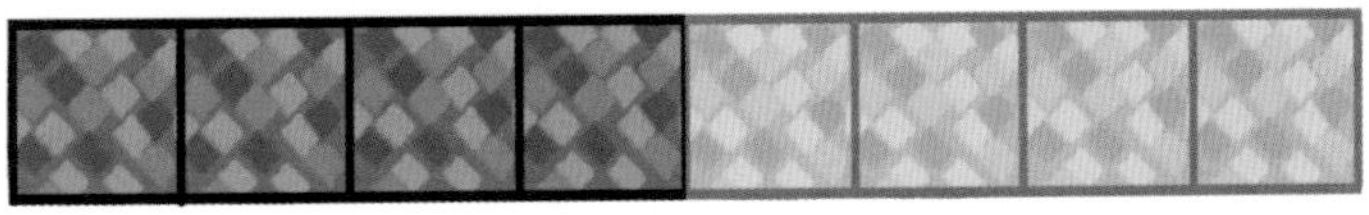 $\dfrac{4}{8}$

10. 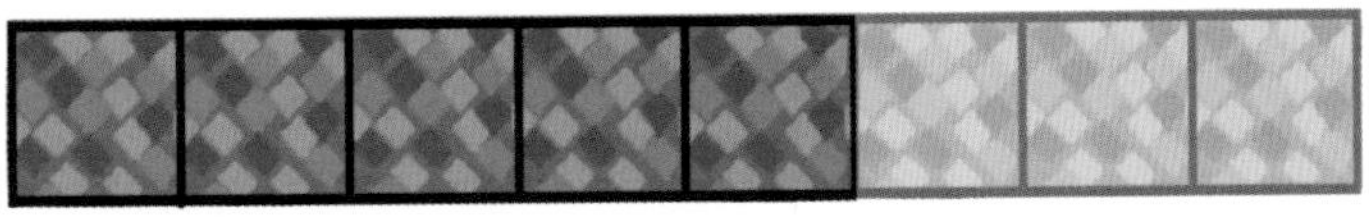 $\dfrac{1}{8}$

ANSWERS

Page 132: Addition By Grouping
2. 16
3. 31
4. 21
5. 17

Page 133: Mystery Message with Addition and Subtraction
2. 3
3. 11
4. 2
5. 13
6. 6
7. 15
8. 7
9. 14
A: Because they have bad STABLE MANNERS

Page 134: Zombie's Guide to Place Value
2. 4 tens 5 ones
3. 2 tens 5 ones
4. 3 tens 1 one
5. 2 tens 8 ones
6. 6 tens 7 ones
7. 5 tens 4 ones

Page 135: Skip Count Challenge
8, 10, 12, 14, 16, 18, 20, 22, 24

Page 136: Telling Time
2. 4:30
3. 11:00
4. 9:30
5. 7:30
6. 5:00

Page 137: Counting Money
2. 23 cents
3. 36 cents
4. 60 cents
5. 37 cents
6. 41 cents
7. 9 cents
Hardcore Mode:
8. 5 nickels

Page 138: Adventures in Geometry
2.
3. 9

Page 139:
4.
5.
6. Hardcore Mode: 1/2

Page 140: Word Problems
1. 1
2. 5
3. 4

Page 141:
4. 8
5. 11
6. 6
7. 9
8. 3

Page 142: Ghast's Guide to Place Value
2. 4 tens, 3 ones
3. 3 tens, 5 ones
4. 2 tens, 9 ones
5. 4 tens, 7 ones
6. 8 tens, 9 ones
7. 6 tens, 3 ones

Page 143: Skip Count Challenge
20, 25, 30, 35, 40, 45, 50, 55, 60

Page 144: All in a Day's Work

2. G
3. F
4. C
5. A
6. B
7. D

Page 145: Time for Matching

Page 146: Learning About Shapes:

1. C
2. A
3. D
4. B

Page 147: Find the Shapes

5. Rectangle
6. Square
7. Circle
8.

Page 148: Addition by Grouping

2. 32
3. 26
4. 28
5. 19

Page 149: Mystery Message with Addition and Subtraction

2. 19
3. 3
4. 14
5. 17
6. 18
7. 13
8. 15
9. 11
10. 8
11. 7
12. 16
A: HE HAD NO BODY TO GO WITH

Page 150: The Enderman Number Challenge

1. D
2. E
3. B
4. A
5. C

Page 151: Skip Count Challenge

30, 40, 50, 60; 80, 90, 100, 110, 120

Page 152: The Tallest Tower

a. 7 Blocks
b. 4 Blocks
c. 6 Blocks

1. A
2. B
3. 3 Blocks

Page 153: The Tallest Tower, cont'd

Tower	Number of Blocks Tall	Color
A	7	GRAY
B	4	GRAY
C	6	GRAY
D		

Page 155: Adventures in Geometry

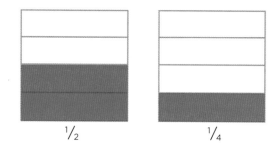

$\frac{1}{2}$ $\frac{1}{4}$

Page 156-157: Word Problems

2. 13 blocks of lava
3. 9 ghasts
4. 22 weapons
5. 17 cookies
6. 14 hunger points
7. 3 items
8. 16 pet cats

Page 158: Creeper's Guide to Place Value

2. Hundreds:7 Tens:6 Ones:0
3. Hundreds:5 Tens:9 Ones:2
4. Hundreds:1 Tens:8 Ones:4
5. Hundreds:5 Tens:3 Ones:2
6. Hundreds:9 Tens:5 Ones:6
7. Hundreds:4 Tens:5 Ones:3

Page 159: Skip Count Challenge

112; 114, 115, 116, 117, 118, 119, 120, 121, 122, 123

Page 160: Mobs and Monsters

	Creeper	Zombie	Ghast	Enderman	Cave Spider	Snow Golem
0 Legs	X					X
2 Legs		X		X		
More than 2 Legs			X		X	

1. 2 legs
2. 4 legs
3. Enderman and Cave Spider

Page 161: Counting Money

1. 13 cents
2. 15 cents
3. 35 cents
4. 29 cents
5. 36 cents

Hardcore Mode: 6. 128 cents, or $1.28

Page 162: Adventures in Geometry: Spot the Shapes

1. Trapezoid
2. Rectangle
3. Square

Page 164: Sandstone Addition

1. 76
2. 97
3. 75
4. 84
5. 97
6. 98
7. 97
8. 74
9. 86
10. 59
11. 36
12. 109

Hidden Message: DESERT

Page 165: Subtraction Mystery Message

1. 13
2. 44
3. 61
4. 15

5. 21

6. 71

7. 11

8. 42

9. 26

10. 53

A: POP MUSIC, OF COURSE

Page **166**: Mob Monster Showdown

1. <

2. >

3. <

4. <

5. >

6. <

7. <

Enderman

Page **167**: Skip Count Challenge

6, 12, 15, 18, 21, 24, 27, 30, 33, 36, 39, 42, 45

Page **168**: Telling Time

2. 4:15

3. 6:10

4. 8:25

5. 3:50

6. 1:55

7. 12:40

8. 9:05

9. 6:45

10. 2:35

11. 1:10

12. 10:25

13. 5:55

14. 6:40

Page **170**: 4 Sides are Better Than 1

1.

2.

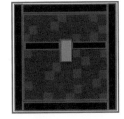

3.

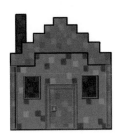

Page **172**: Addition & Subtraction Mystery Number

1. 3

2. 7

3. 10

4. 8

5. 6

6. 14

7. 7

8. 3

9. 7

Page **173**: Mystery Message with Addition Using Regrouping

1. 54

2. 96

3. 41

4. 40

5. 44

6. 31

7. 73

8. 93

9. 70

10. 72

A: ONE. AFTER THAT IT'S NOT EMPTY.

Page **174**: Pigman's Guide to Place Value

1. 3

2. 9

3. 2

4. 8

5. 4

6. 1

7. 9

Page **175**: Skip Count Challenge

12; 20, 24, 28, 32, 36, 40, 44, 48, 52, 56, 64, 68

Page 176: Animal Tally

1. 6
2. Steve
3. 5
4. 7

Page 177: Weapons Tally

1. 10
2. 2
3. 10
4. Steve

Page 178: Spot the Shapes

1.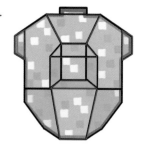

2.

Page 179: Adventures in Geometry: Spot the Shape

1. Cube
2. Quadrilateral
3. Octagon
4. Sphere
5. Oval

Page 180: Word Problems

2. 19 mushrooms
3. 11 snow golems
4. 14 zombie villagers
5. 18 eyes of Ender
6. 30 fireballs
7. 40 cobblestone blocks

Page 182: Iron Golem's Guide to Place Value

2. 2
3. 5
4. 8
5. 8
6. 2
7. 1

Page 183: Skip Count

200; 400, 500, 600, 700, 800, 900, 1000

Page 184: Telling Time

2. 2:25
3. 7:50
4. 8:05
5. 9:35
6. 1:15

Page 185: Counting Money

2. 60 cents
3. 39 cents
4. 42 cents
5. 83 cents

Hardcore Mode:

6. Dime

Page 186-187: Geometry

1.   2.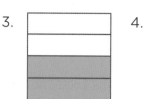

3.   4.

5. Two fourths
6. $\frac{1}{8}$
7. $\frac{2}{8}$
8. $\frac{3}{8}$
9. $\frac{4}{8}$
10. $\frac{5}{8}$

MATH FOR MINECRAFTERS

Adventures in Multiplication & Division

A NOTE TO PARENTS

When you want to reinforce classroom skills at home, it's crucial to have kid-friendly learning materials. This *Math for Minecrafters* workbook transforms math practice into an irresistible adventure complete with diamond swords, zombies, skeletons, and creepers. That means less arguing over homework and more fun overall.

Math for Minecrafters is also fully aligned with National Common Core Standards for 3rd and 4th grade math. What does that mean, exactly? All of the problems in this book correspond to what your child is expected to learn in school. This eliminates confusion and builds confidence for greater homework-time success!

As an added benefit to parents, the pages of this workbook are color-coded to help you target specific skill areas as needed. Each color represents one of the four categories of Common Core math instruction. Use the chart below to guide you in understanding the different skills being taught at your child's school and to pinpoint areas where he or she may need extra practice.

BLUE   Operations and Algebraic Thinking

PINK   Numbers and Operations in Base 10

GREEN   Measurement and Data

ORANGE   Geometry

As the workbook progresses, the math problems become more advanced. Encourage your child to progress at his or her own pace. Learning is best when students are challenged, but not frustrated. What's most important is that your Minecrafter is engaged in his or her own learning.

Whether it's the joy of seeing their favorite game characters on every page or the thrill of solving challenging problems just like Steve and Alex, there is something in this workbook to entice even the most reluctant math student.

Happy adventuring!

MULTIPLICATION BY GROUPING

Write the multiplication sentence that matches the picture.
Then solve the equation.

Example:

1.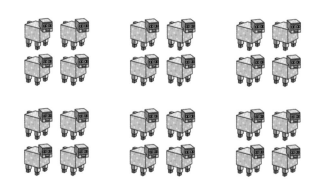

Answer:

$$\underline{2} \times \underline{10} = \underline{20}$$

2. _____ x _____ = _____

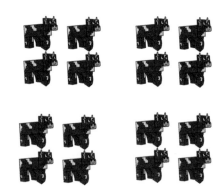

3. _____ x _____ = _____

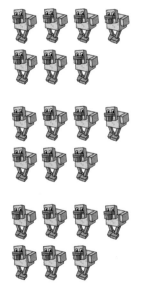

4. _____ x _____ = _____

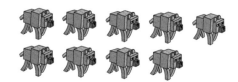

5. _____ x _____ = _____

MYSTERY MESSAGE
WITH MULTIPLICATION

Multiply. Then use the letters to fill in the blanks below and reveal the answer to the joke.

1. 4 x 8 = 32 A

2. 2 x 6 = ___ D

3. 6 x 3 = ___ Y

4. 3 x 8 = ___ C

5. 7 x 5 = ___ S

6. 8 x 5 = ___ O

7. 8 x 2 = ___ E

8. 9 x 6 = ___ R

9. 10 x 3 = ___ T

Q: Where does a baby creeper go when his parents are at work?

COPY THE LETTERS FROM THE ANSWERS ABOVE TO FIND OUT.

He goes ___ ___
        30 40

___ A ___ ___ ___ A ___ ___
12 32 18 35 24 32 54 16

ZOMBIE'S GUIDE TO PLACE VALUE

Write the number on each zombie in expanded form in the space provided.

Example:

1.
1,360

Answer:

1,000 + 300 + 60 + 0

2.
4,672

_____

3.
2,798

_____

4.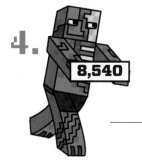
8,540

_____

5.
3,151

_____

6.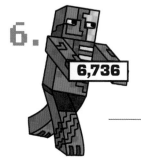
6,736

_____

7.
5,459

_____

MATH FACTS CHALLENGE

Find the pattern and fill in the empty spaces to help Alex escape the zombie.

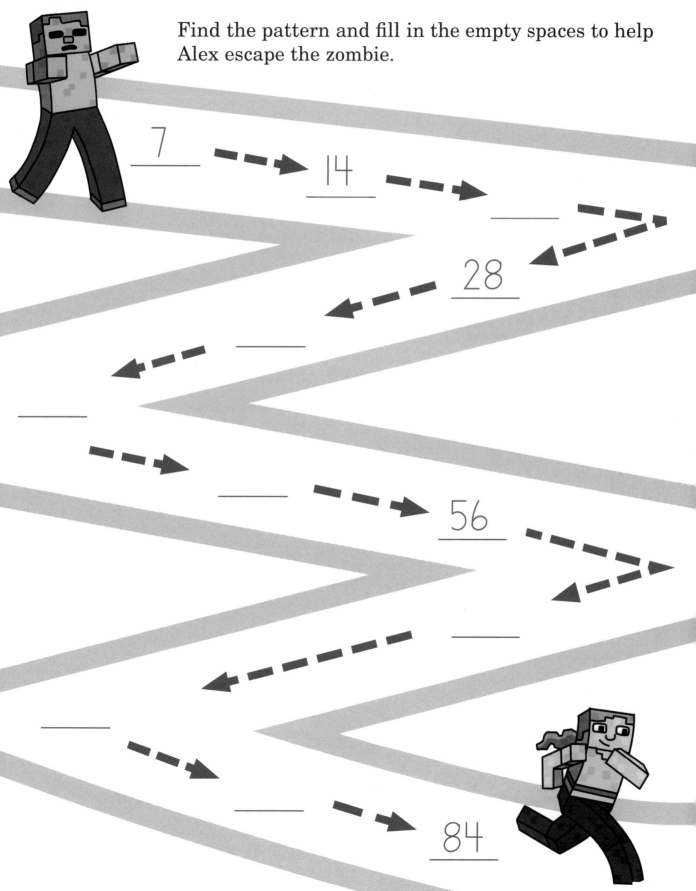

7 → 14 → ___ → 28 → ___ → ___ → ___ → 56 → ___ → ___ → ___ → 84

TELLING TIME

Look at the clocks below and write the time in the space provided:

Example:

1.

Answer: 2:15

2.

Answer: _____

3.

Answer: _____

4.

Answer: _____

5.

Answer: _____

6.

Answer: _____

THE TRADING TABLE

The villagers have emeralds to give Alex in exchange for her food items. Look at the table below to solve the problems that follow.

FARMER	🟢	🟢	🟢	🟢			
LIBRARIAN	🟢	🟢					
BLACKSMITH	🟢	🟢	🟢				
BUTCHER	🟢	🟢	🟢	🟢	🟢	🟢	

Write the amount of emeralds next to each villager using the table above.

1 pile of emeralds = 8 emeralds.

1. The **farmer** villager has _____ .

2. The **librarian** villager has _____ .

3. The **blacksmith** villager has _____ .

4. The **butcher** villager has _____ .

5. Which villagers have more emeralds than the **blacksmith** villager? _____

6. Which villager has the least amount of emeralds? _____

7. The **librarian** wants to have as many emeralds as the **butcher**. Which villager's collection does he need to add to his? _____

GEOMETRY SKILLS PRACTICE

How many items are in each array? Count the number of items in one row and one column. Write a multiplication sentence to find the answer.

Example:

1. <u>2</u> x <u>5</u> = <u>10</u>

2. ____ x ____ = ____

3. ____ x ____ = ____

4. ____ x ____ = ____

5. ____ x ____ = ____

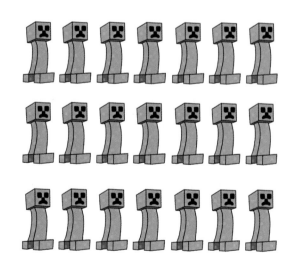

6. ___ x ___ = ___

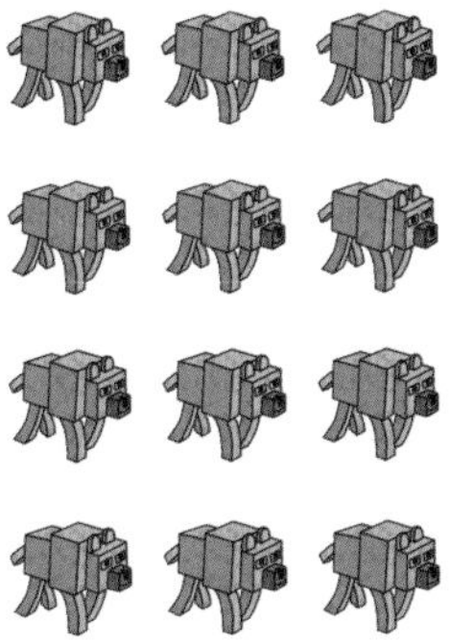

7. ___ x ___ = ___

8. ___ x ___ = ___

9. ___ x ___ = ___

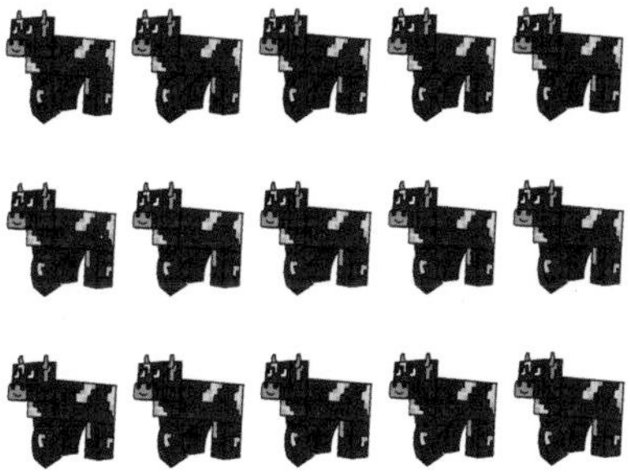

HARDCORE MODE: Try this hardcore math challenge!

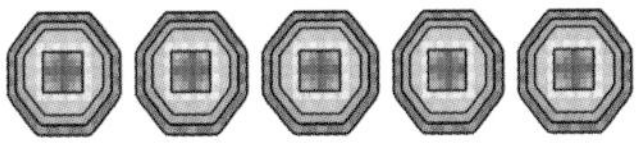

___ x ___ = ___ + ___ = ___

MULTIPLICATION WORD PROBLEMS

Read the problem carefully. Draw a picture or write a number sentence to help you solve the problem.

Example:

1. A creeper blows up 2 cows every time it explodes. How many cows will be killed by 3 exploding creepers?

Answer: 6 cows

$3 \times 2 = 6$

2. In order to make 1 cake, you need 3 buckets of milk. How many buckets of milk do you need to make 2 cakes?

Answer: _____

3. One block of wood is enough to make 4 planks of wood. If you have 4 blocks of wood, how many planks can you make?

Answer: _____

4. One ocelot drops 3 experience orbs for you to collect. How many experience orbs can you collect from 6 ocelots?

Answer: _____

204

5. You need 6 sandstone blocks to craft 1 set of stairs. How many sandstone blocks do you need to build 7 sets of stairs?

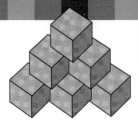

Answer: _____

6. One cow drops 3 pieces of raw beef. How many pieces of raw beef can you get from 4 cows?

Answer: _____

7. One full day in the game world is the same as 20 minutes in the real world. If you spend 5 days in Alex's world, how many real-world minutes go by?

Answer: _____

8. Steve needs 9 fish to tame an ocelot. How many fish does he need to tame 3 ocelots?

Answer: _____

9. It takes 4 bottles of potion to survive a hostile mob attack. How many bottles of potion do you need to survive 6 mob attacks?

Answer: _____

GHAST'S GUIDE TO PLACE VALUE

Answer the multiplication questions below.
Then round to the closest ten.

Solve It!   **Round It!**

1. 2 x 3 = 6   10

2. 4 x 9 = ___   ___

3. 6 x 8 = ___   ___

4. 3 x 5 = ___   ___

5. 7 x 4 = ___   ___

6. 8 x 5 = ___   ___

7. 9 x 7 = ___   ___

MATH FACTS CHALLENGE

Count by 4 and practice your math facts to help
Steve escape the wither!

4

8

48

MINUTE HAND MYSTERY

A computer glitch erased the minute hands from these clocks! Solve the problem to find out how many minutes have passed, then draw in the minute hand.

Solve it.

Draw it.

1. 10 ÷ 2 = ___5___ minutes

2. 15 x 3 = _____ minutes

3. 60 ÷ 4 = _____ minutes

4. 20 x 2 = _____ minutes

5. 11 x 5 = _____ minutes

6. 75 ÷ 3 = _____ minutes

EQUAL TRADE

This librarian villager loves trading for new coins. Figure out the right number of coins to trade so that you don't lose any money in the deal.

1. How many **pennies** equal 1 dime?

Answer: _____

2. How many **nickels** equal 1 quarter?

Answer: _____

3. How many **pennies** equal 3 nickels?

Answer: _____

4. How many **quarters** equal a dollar?

Answer: _____

5. How many **dimes** equal 2 quarters?

Answer: _____

ADVENTURES IN GEOMETRY

Which of these gaming images are symmetrical? Circle them.

Symmetrical = an object that can be divided with a line into two matching halves.

CREATIVE MODE

Complete the other half of this drawing to make it as symmetrical as possible:

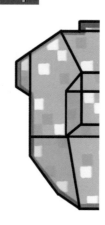

SHELTER GEOMETRY

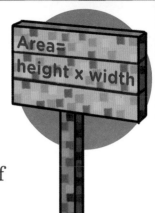

Area = height x width

Alex and Steve have been working all afternoon to build a new shelter out of redstone blocks.

1. Calculate the area of Alex's wall:

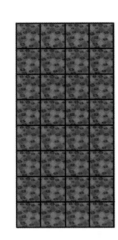

_____ x _____ = _____

2. Calculate the area of Steve's wall:

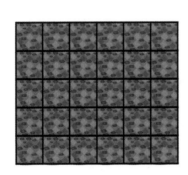

_____ x _____ = _____

3. Which player's wall has the greatest area? _____

4. How many more blocks did that player use? _____

5. If you combine their two walls, what would the area of their new, larger wall be? _____

MULTIPLICATION BY GROUPING

Count each group of 3, then finish the equation to find the answer.

1. _____ × 3 = _____

2. _____ × 3 = _____

3. _____ × 3 = _____

4. _____ × 3 = _____

5. _____ × 3 = _____

MYSTERY MESSAGE
WITH MULTIPLICATION AND DIVISION

Solve the problems below to find out which number matches with which letter. Then put the correct letters into the message to answer the riddle!

1. $234 \div 2 =$ _117_ _E_

2. $34 \times 3 =$ _____ _O_

3. $77 \times 4 =$ _____ _H_

4. $434 \div 7 =$ _____ _R_

5. $165 \times 5 =$ _____ _B_

6. $924 \div 4 =$ _____ _N_

7. $201 \times 3 =$ _____ _I_

Q: What mysterious character looks like Steve but has glowing white eyes?

COPY THE LETTERS FROM THE ANSWERS ABOVE TO FIND OUT.

308   117   62   102   825   62   603   231   117

ENDERMAN'S GUIDE TO PLACE VALUE

Solve the multiplication equations below. Match each answer to the correct place value description on the right.

1. 12 x 4 = 36 ___

2. 8 x 8 = ___

3. 9 x 9 = ___

4. 10 x 20 = ___

5. 8 x 9 = ___

6. 11 x 5 = ___

7. 5 x 6 = ___

A. 2 hundreds

B. 6 ones

C. 7 tens

D. 3 tens

E. 4 ones

F. 8 tens

G. 5 ones

SKIP COUNT CHALLENGE

Thanks to the lure enchantment, you catch 9 pufferfish every time you go fishing! Pretty soon, you'll have enough to tame your ocelot. Count by 9 to find out how many pufferfish you'll catch at the end of the day.

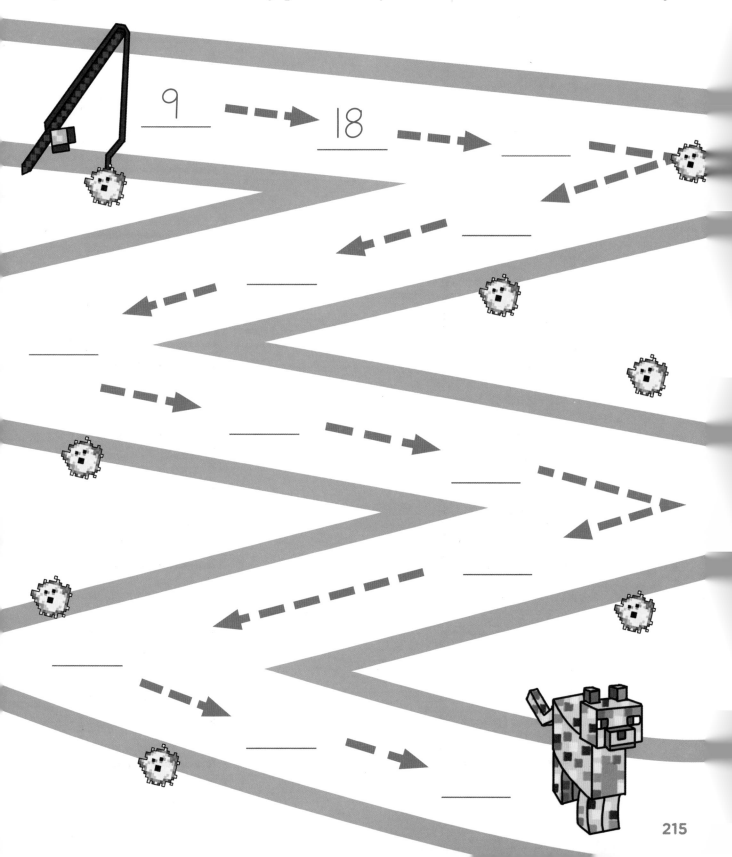

9 ⟶ 18

TELLING TIME

The mooshroom is teaching his baby how to tell time, but he needs your help. Help the baby mooshroom by writing down the correct time next to each clock.

Example:

1.

Answer: 3:25

2.

Answer: _____

3.

Answer: _____

4.

Answer: _____

5.

Answer: _____

6.

Answer: _____

7.

Answer: _____

8.

Answer: _____

SPAWN EGG CHALLENGE

Solve the equations next to each colored bucket to find out how many exploding creepers will soon be hatching from the buckets. Then run!

1. 27 x 5 = _____

2. 120 ÷ 6 = _____

3. 94 x 2 = _____

4. 39 x 2 = _____

5. 320 ÷ 8 = _____

6. 53 x 4 = _____

7. Which colored bucket has the most creeper eggs? _____

8. Which two colored buckets, when combined, add up to 228 creeper eggs? _____ and _____

HARDCORE MODE: Try this hardcore math challenge!

9. What is the sum of all the creeper eggs? _____

EQUAL PARTS CHALLENGE

Use a ruler or the edge of a piece of paper to help you draw partitions in the shapes below.

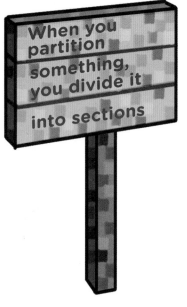

When you partition something, you divide it into sections

1. The first gold ingot below is partitioned, or divided, into two equal parts with the red line.

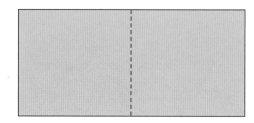

There is another way to divide this gold ingot into two equal, symmetrical parts.
Draw it below:

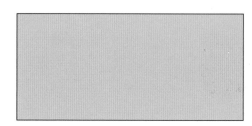

Use your pencil to shade in one of the pieces above.
What fraction describes this picture? _____

2. Partition the iron ingot into **3** equal shares in two different ways.

Use your pencil to shade in one of the pieces above. What fraction describes this picture? _____

3. Partition the iron ingot into **4** equal shares in two different ways.

Use your pencil to shade in one of the pieces above. What fraction describes this picture? _____

MYSTERY MESSAGE WITH MULTIPLICATION

Solve each multiplication equation below. Use the answers to solve the riddle.

1. 57
   ×9
   ‾‾‾
   513

2. 72
   ×5

3. 27
   ×9

4. 57
   ×6

5. 41
   ×6

6. 46
   ×8

A   G   Q   S   N   U

7. 84
   ×4

8. 26
   ×9

9. 50
   ×7

10. 78
    ×6

11. 41
    ×8

E   C   D   I   R

Q: What is Steve's favorite type of dancing?

COPY THE LETTERS FROM THE ANSWERS ABOVE TO FIND OUT.

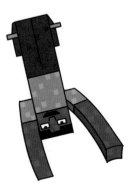

342	243	368	513	328	336

350	513	246	234	468	246	360

MULTIPLICATION AND DIVISION MYSTERY NUMBER

Some hacker has replaced a number from each of the below equations with a TNT block. Use multiplication and division to solve for the missing numbers.

1. 3 × = 24   = 8

2. ÷ 8 = 6   =

3. 120 ÷ = 12   =

4. 3 × = 21   =

5. 45 ÷ = 9   =

6. × 9 = 36   =

7. 12 ÷ = 3   =

8. × 12 = 60   =

9. 27 ÷ = 9   =

10. 42 ÷ = 6   =

221

SNOW GOLEM'S NUMBER CHALLENGE

Match the Snow Golem with the description of the number.

1. Hundreds: **1** Tens: **2** Ones: **9**

642÷2

2. Hundreds: **3** Tens: **2** Ones: **1**

51x8

3. Hundreds: **1** Tens: **7** Ones: **5**

26x9

4. Hundreds: **4** Tens: **0** Ones: **8**

875÷5

5. Hundreds: **2** Tens: **3** Ones: **4**

43 x 3

SKIP COUNT CHALLENGE

A rare but hostile chicken jockey is headed your way!
Solve the equation and count by the answer to escape.

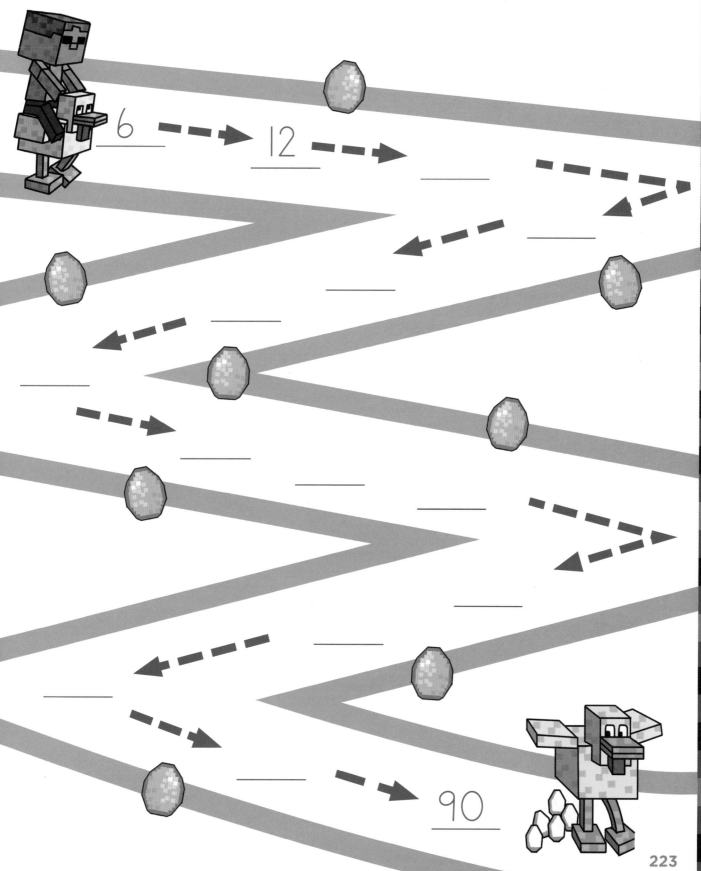

6 → 12 → ___ →
___
___
___
___ →
___
___
___
___
___ →
___
___ →
___ → 90

223

CREATING POTIONS

Use the recipes below to figure out the number of items needed to make more of each potion.

1. = 3 awkward potions + 3 glistering melons

= _____ awkward potions +

_____ glistering melons

2. = 2 awkward potions + 5 sugars

= _____ awkward potions + _____ sugars

3. = 7 golden carrots + 9 nether warts

= _____ golden carrots +

_____ nether warts

INVISIBILITY POTION FORMULA

4. 🧪 = 4 potions of night vision + 7 fermented spider eyes

🧪🧪🧪🧪🧪
🧪🧪🧪🧪 = _____ potions of night vision +

_____ fermented spider eyes

INVISIBILITY POTION INGREDIENTS TABLE

Use the formula above to determine how much you need of each ingredient below. The first one is done for you.

Night Vision Potion	8			
Fermented Spider Eyes				

ADVENTURES IN GEOMETRY: PERIMETER AND AREA

Steve is building new rooms in his house. Multiply the number of blocks to help him find the perimeter and area of the walls.

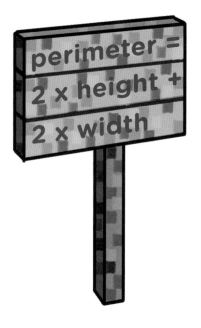

perimeter =
2 x height +
2 x width

1. Perimeter = _____

If Steve doubles the height of this wall,

what would the new perimeter be? _____

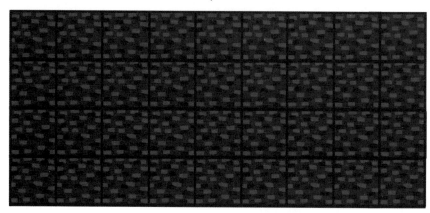

2. Perimeter = _____

If Steve destroys the right half of this wall,

what would the new perimeter be? _____

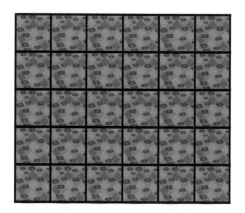

3. Perimeter = _____

Alex built a wall twice as wide as this one.

What was the perimeter of her new wall?

_____

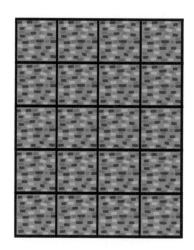

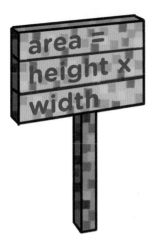

area = height x width

4. Area = _____

If Steve doubles the height of this wall, what would the new area be? _____

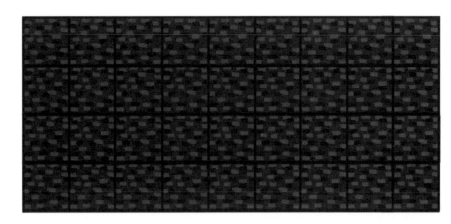

5. Area = _____

If Steve destroys the right half of this wall, what would the new area be? _____

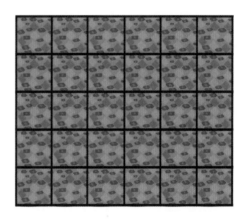

6. Area = _____

Alex built a wall twice as big as this one. What was the area of her wall? _____

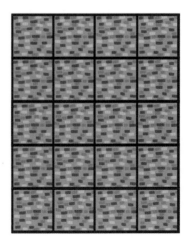

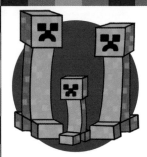

WORD PROBLEMS

Use multiplication and division to solve these word problems.

1. Alex is planning to get carrots for her horses. She has 32 horses and each horse needs 8 carrots a day. How many carrots does she need to feed the horses each day?

Answer: _____

2. Steve plants melon seeds in his garden. He figures out that 3 seeds make one melon. If his garden made 48 melons, how many seeds did he plant?

Answer: _____

3. You destroy 12 Endermen with your iron sword! If each Enderman drops 4 Ender pearls when he dies, how many pearls do you collect?

Answer: _____

4. Baby zombies are spawning! You spot 16 little green zombies total. If you encounter 3 more groups of 16 baby zombies, how many zombies will you encounter in all?

Answer: _____

5. Steve needs to feed his mooshrooms and baby mooshrooms. Each adult needs 2 wheat items, while each baby needs just 1 wheat item. If he has 12 adult mooshrooms and 5 baby mooshrooms, how many wheat items does he need to feed them?

Answer: _____

6. Escape the charged creepers! If it takes you 6 minutes to row your wooden boat 9 feet, how long do you estimate it will take you to row across a river that is 54 feet wide?

Answer: _____

7. Steve has 68 blocks of redstone that he needs to transport to his house. If 2 blocks can fit in his mining cart during each trip, how many trips will he have to take to move them all?

Answer: _____

8. You want to make cookies for all of your favorite players. You need 2 wheat items to make each batch of cookies. If you make 63 batches of cookies, how many wheat items do you need?

Answer: _____

PLACE VALUE

Match the answer to each equation on the left with the number of emeralds on the right to help Steve calculate how many emeralds total he mined on a certain day.

1. 3 x 12 x 5 = ____

2. 9 x 22 x 4 = ____

3. 15 x 3 x 9 = ____

4. 7 x 14 x 6 = ____

5. 6 x 24 x 4 = ____

6. 2 x 35 x 9 = ____

7. 13 x 8 x 2 = ____

A  405

B.  630

C.  576

D. 180

E.  588

F.  208

G. 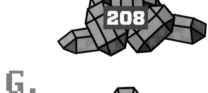 792

GHASTLY NUMBER CHALLENGE

Match the answer to the Ghast's equation on the right with the correct place value description on the left.

1. Hundreds: **9** Tens: **1** Ones: **2**

44 x 7

2. Hundreds: **6** Tens: **7** Ones: **2**

76 x 10

3. Hundreds: **3** Tens: **0** Ones: **8**

24 x 38

4. Hundreds: **2** Tens: **2** Ones: **0**

2200 ÷ 10

5. Hundreds: **7** Tens: **6** Ones: **0**

498 ÷ 2

6. Hundreds: **2** Tens: **4** Ones: **9**

42 x 16

7. Hundreds: **5** Tens: **2** Ones: **0**

26 x 20

MOB MEASUREMENTS

Find out how many inches tall each mob is using multiplication and addition.

1 foot = 12 inches

Example:

1.

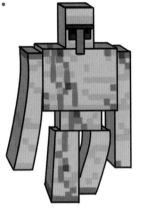

Iron Golem

3 feet, 4 inches

12 x 3 = __36__ inches

36 + 4 = __40__ inches tall

2.

Zombie

2 feet, 6 inches

Height in inches = _____

3.

Skeleton

3 feet, 1 inch

Height in inches = _____

4.

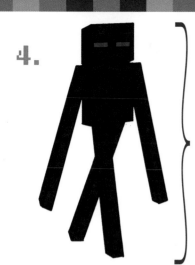

Enderman

4 feet, 3 inches

Height in inches = _____

5.

Rabbit

1 foot, 6 inches

Height in inches = _____

METRIC MEASUREMENTS

Complete the chart using the formula provided.

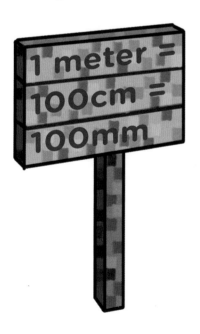

1 meter =
100cm =
100mm

	Length in meters	Length in cm	Length in mm
	2	200	2,000
		400	
	1.5		1,500
			2,500
	1		

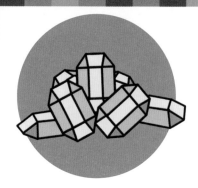

ADVENTURES IN GEOMETRY

Identify the angle shown in each picture as acute, right, or obtuse.

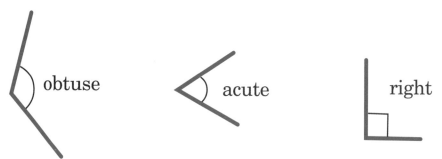

obtuse   acute   right

1. _____   2. _____

3. _____   4. _____

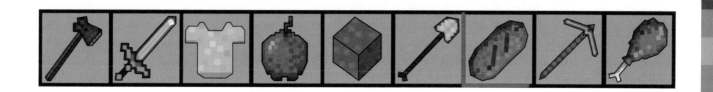

5. _____

6. _____

7. _____

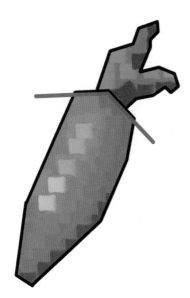

8. _____

9. _____

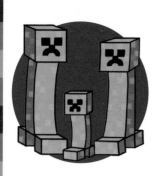

MULTIPLICATION AND DIVISION MYSTERY NUMBER

A troublesome creeper has replaced a number in each equation with a creeper spawn egg! Use multiplication and division to determine the missing number.

1. $217 \div$ 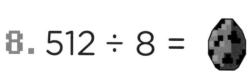 $= 31$ 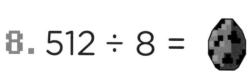 $=$ _____

2. 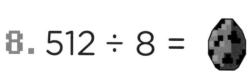 $\div 5 = 85$ 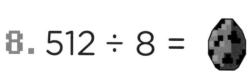 $=$ _____

3. $548 \div 4 =$ 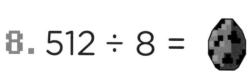   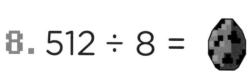 $=$ _____

4. $424 \div$ 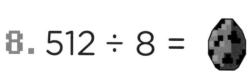 $= 4$ 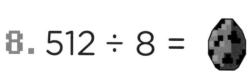 $=$ _____

5. $48 \div 6 =$ 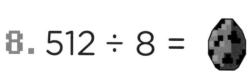   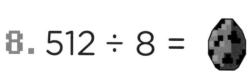 $=$ _____

6. 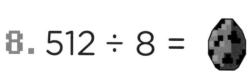 $\div 3 = 126$ 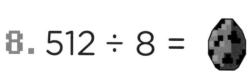 $=$ _____

7. $72 \div$ 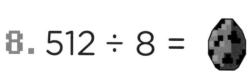 $= 9$ 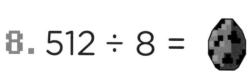 $=$ _____

8. $512 \div 8 =$ 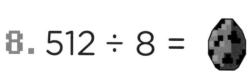   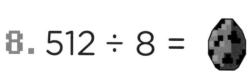 $=$ _____

9. $9 \times$ 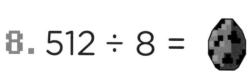 $= 702$ 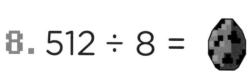 $=$ _____

MYSTERY MESSAGE
WITH MULTIPLICATION AND DIVISION

Solve the multiplication and division problems below. Then write the letters in the blank spaces at the bottom of the page to get the answer to the joke!

1. 892 ÷ 2 = _____   G

2. 45 x 8 = _____   B

3. 623 ÷ 7 = _____   I

4. 1122 ÷ 6 = _____   N

5. 91 x 9 = _____   O

6. 230 x 4 = _____   X

Q: What is a Minecrafter's favorite sport?

COPY THE LETTERS FROM THE ANSWERS ABOVE TO FIND OUT.

Answer:

360 819 920 89 187 446

SKELETON'S GUIDE TO PLACE VALUE

Solve the division equations below to fill in the empty place value box beside each one.

1. $917 \div 7 =$ ___

Hundreds

2. $255 \div 5 =$ ___

Ones

3. $1{,}473 \div 3 =$ ___

Tens

4. $336 \div 24 =$ ___

Ones

5. $425 \div 5 =$ ___

Tens

6. $2{,}004 \div 4 =$ ___

Hundreds

7. $1{,}602 \div 6 =$ ___

Ones

SKIP COUNT CHALLENGE

A mob of zombie villagers has discovered you in the forest! Figure out the number pattern and fill in the blanks to complete the path before the villagers can catch you.

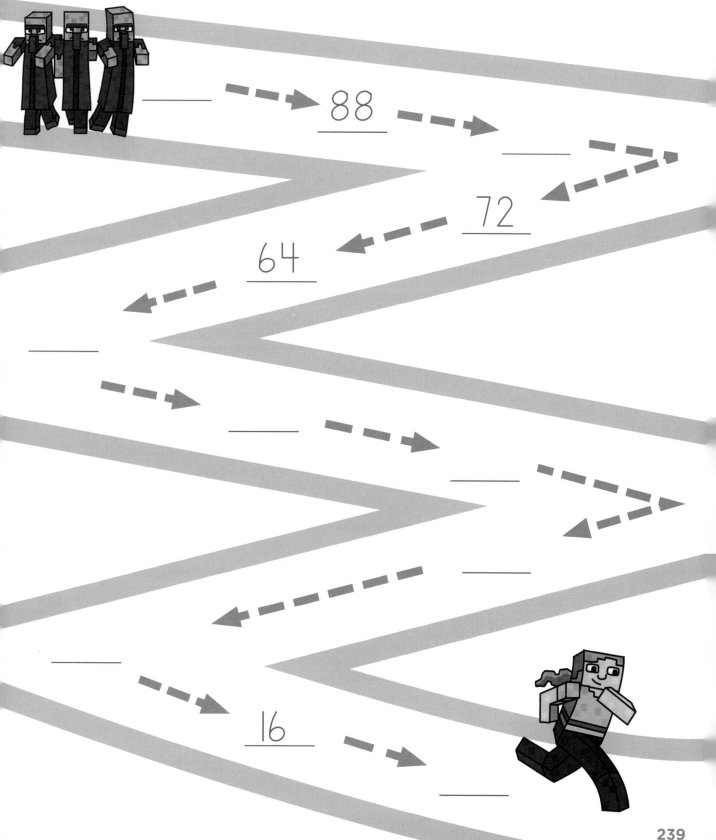

_____ → 88 → _____ → 72 → 64 → _____ → _____ → _____ → _____ → _____ → 16 → _____

ANIMAL TALLY

Use the six clues below to help you fill in the chart on the right-hand page.

1. If Steve can fit 6 chickens at each of his farms and he has 2 farms full of chickens, plus 2 extra chickens that he keeps in his house, how many chickens total does he have?

2. If Alex has 4 times as many chickens as Steve, how many does she have?

3. If Steve has 51 horses and Alex has $\frac{1}{3}$ the amount that he has, how many horses does she have?

4. If Steve has 13 sheep and Alex has 4 times that number of sheep, how many sheep does she have?

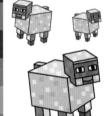

5. If Steve has 5 groups of 20 cows and horses combined, how many cows does he have?

6. If Alex has $\frac{1}{7}$ the amount of cows as Steve, how many cows does she have total?

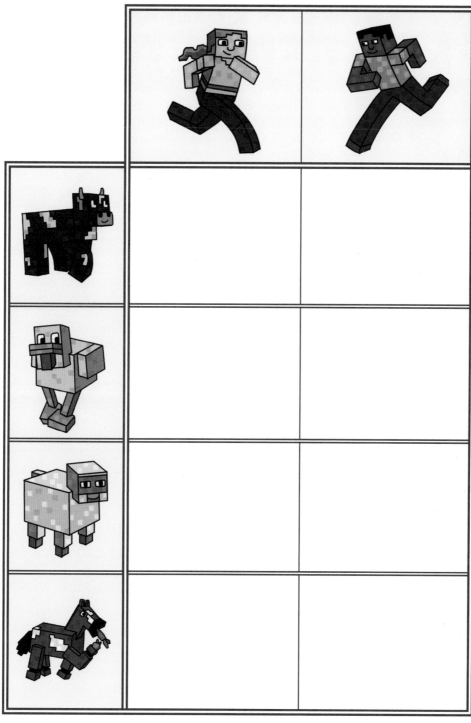

ADVENTURES IN GEOMETRY

Label the red lines on each image as parallel, perpendicular, or intersecting.

 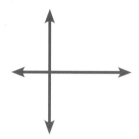 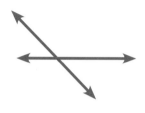

Parallel Lines **Perpendicular Lines** **Intersecting Lines**

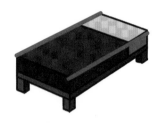

1. _____

2. _____

3. _____

4. _____

5. _____

6. _____

7. _____

WORD PROBLEMS

Use multiplication, division, addition, and subtraction to solve these word problems.

1. Each pickaxe in your inventory bar digs up 5 diamonds before breaking. You dig up 4,650 diamonds total. How many pickaxes did you use?

2. You are hiding from 42 hostile mobs. Half of them are 8-legged cave spiders. The other half are 2-legged skeletons. How many legs are there in this angry group of mobs?

3. Steve has a collection of mining carts. Each cart can hold 7 redstone blocks inside. How many carts does Steve have if he can hold 91 redstone blocks total?

4. Zombie villagers have been stomping through your garden, crushing your flowers. If you had 400 flowers in your garden last week and the zombie villagers have crushed $\frac{1}{4}$ of them, how many do you now have?

5. Every year a villager near you adds 2 feet to the height of her house. If her house is currently 10 feet high, how high will it be in 7 years?

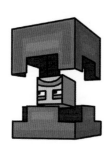

6. You have stumbled upon a wall of purpur blocks, and soon discover that every third block has a hostile shulker hidden inside it. If there are 1,260 purpur blocks total in the wall, how many shulkers are there?

7. You and 4 other players are trying to cross a river in the jungle biome. You figure out that 12 lily pads can hold the weight of 2 players. How many lily pads will it take for all 5 of you to cross the river?

GIANT'S GUIDE TO PLACE VALUE

Answer the multiplication and division questions below. Write the correct digit in the place value box.

1. 3416 ÷ 4 = _____

Tens

2. 2200 ÷ 10 = _____

Hundreds

3. 19,450 ÷ 5 = _____

Thousands

4. 783 x 9 = _____

Ones

5. 400,325 ÷ 5 = _____

Ten Thousands

6. 375 ÷ 3 = _____

Hundreds

7. 791,000 ÷ 7 = _____

Hundred Thousands

SKIP COUNT CHALLENGE

You've stumbled upon a pigman hiding in the bushes! Find the pattern to fill in the blanks to finish the path and get to your protective armor.

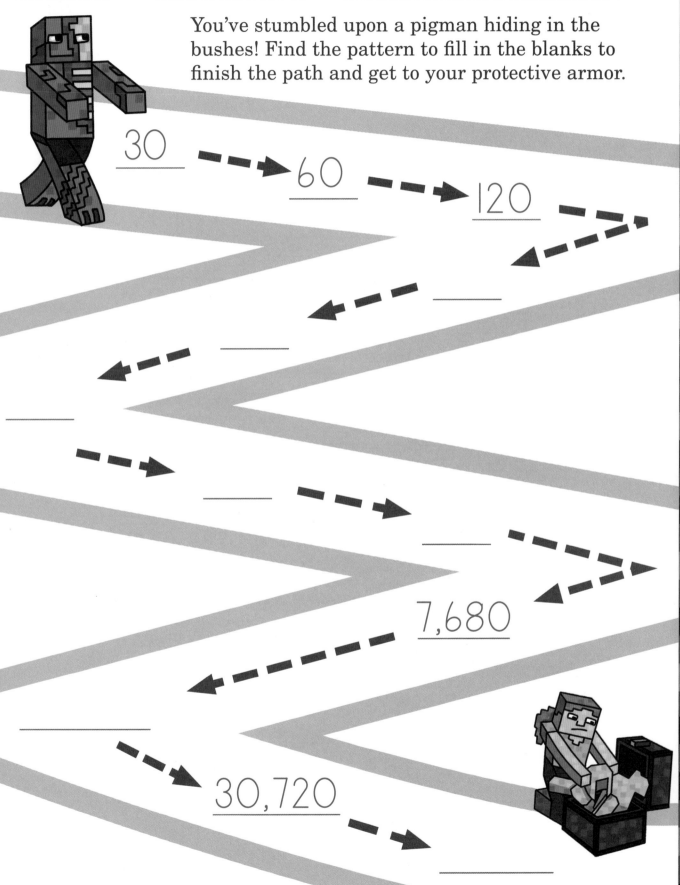

30 → 60 → 120 → ___ → ___ → ___ → ___ → ___ → 7,680 → ___ → 30,720 → ___

COMPARING FRACTIONS

Can a wolf take down a zombie? Compare the fractions and circle the one that is greater to determine who wins in each battle.

HINT: Draw two same-sized boxes and shade them in to help you compare.

1. $\frac{2}{3}$ $\quad$ $\frac{1}{6}$

2. $\frac{3}{4}$ $\quad$ $\frac{7}{8}$

3. $\frac{1}{4}$ $\quad$ $\frac{1}{3}$

4. $\frac{6}{20}$ $\quad$ $\frac{1}{5}$

5. $\frac{6}{12}$ $\quad$ $\frac{4}{6}$

6. $\frac{1}{3}$ $\quad$ $\frac{4}{8}$

7. $\frac{3}{4}$ $\quad$ $\frac{1}{2}$

8. $\frac{1}{3}$ $\quad$ $\frac{5}{6}$

Who won the most battles overall? _____

EQUAL FRACTIONS

One week in Steve's world is 140 minutes in real life! Use multiplication and division to fill in the chart and find out how much time Steve spends on each activity.

	Minutes out of a half day (10 minutes)	Minutes out of a day (20 minutes)	Minutes out of a week (140 minutes)
farming	$^1/_{10}$	$^2/_{20}$	$^{14}/_{140}$
fighting	$^3/_{10}$	$—/_{20}$	$—/_{140}$
crafting	$^2/_{10}$	$—/_{20}$	$—/_{140}$
mining	$—/_{10}$	$—/_{20}$	$^{56}/_{140}$

What does Steve spend most of his week doing? _____

GEOMETRY WORD PROBLEMS

Solve the problems using multiplication and division.

1. If Steve builds a square wall out of lapis lazuli and the wall has an area of 64 square feet, how many feet long is each side of the wall?

2. A Minecrafter's bookcase is shaped like a cube. If each side of that cube is 4 feet long, how many bookcases can you squeeze onto a 144-square-foot floor?

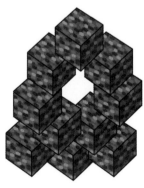

3. Alex has a rectangular fenced-in area that is 4,500 square feet. If the length of the fence is 150 feet, how wide is it?

4. Steve walks the perimeter of his house twice each day to check for zombies and creepers. If all the sides of his house are 24 feet long, how many feet does Steve walk every day?

5. Alex's treasure chest measures 12 feet by 16 feet. She can fit 4 emeralds in every square foot. How many emeralds can she fit in the chest?

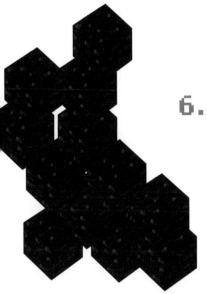

6. Steve built a rectangular obsidian wall that has a perimeter of 20 feet. If the wall is 2 feet long, how wide is it?

7. Steve wants to fit all 18 of his pet cats inside his house. If each cat needs 2 square feet to move freely, how long do the sides of his square house have to be?

ANSWER KEY

Page 196: Multiplication by Grouping

2. 4 x 4 = 16 cows
3. 3 x 7 = 21 chickens
4. 1 x 9 = 9 wolves
5. 6 x 4 = 24 sheep

Page 197: Mystery Message with Multiplication

2. 12
3. 18
4. 24
5. 35
6. 40
7. 16
8. 54
9. 30

Answer: He goes TO DAYSCARE

Page 198: Zombie's Guide to Place Value

2. 4,000 + 600 + 70 + 2
3. 2,000 + 700 + 90 + 8
4. 8,000 + 500 + 40 + 0
5. 3,000 + 100 + 50 + 1
6. 6,000 + 700 + 30 + 6
7. 5,000 + 400 + 50 + 9

Page 199: Math Facts Challenge

7, 14, 21, 28, 35, 42, 49, 56, 63, 70, 77, 84

Page 200: Telling Time

2. 4:40
3. 11:05
4. 9:20
5. 7:10
6. 4:50

Page 201: The Trading Table

1. 32 emeralds
2. 16 emeralds
3. 24 emeralds
4. 48 emeralds
5. The farmer and the butcher.
6. The librarian.
7. The farmer's collection.

Pages 202–203: Geometry Skills Practice

2. 3 x 6 = 18 potions
3. 4 x 4 = 16 experience orbs
4. 2 x 7 = 14 clocks
5. 3 x 7 = 21 creepers
6. 4 x 3 = 12 wolves
7. 1 x 9 = 9 zombies
8. 2 x 6 = 12 spiders
9. 3 x 5 = 15 cows

Hardcore Mode: 7 x 7 = 49 + 5 = 54 experience orbs

Pages 204-205: Multiplication Word Problems

2. 6 buckets
3. 16 planks
4. 18 experience orbs
5. 42 blocks
6. 12 pieces
7. 100 minutes
8. 27 fish
9. 24 bottles

Page 206: Ghast's Guide to Place Value

2. 36, 40
3. 48, 50
4. 15, 20
5. 28, 30
6. 40, 40
7. 63, 60

Page 207: Math Facts Challenge

4, 8, 12, 16, 20, 24, 28, 32, 36, 40, 44, 48

Page 208: Minute Hand Mystery

2. 45 minutes

3. 15 minutes

4. 40 minutes

5. 55 minutes

6. 25 minutes

Page 209: Equal Trade

1. 10 pennies
2. 5 nickels
3. 15 pennies
4. 4 quarters
5. 5 dimes

Page 210: Adventures in Geometry

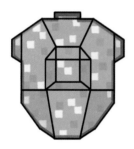

Page 211: Shelter Geometry

1. Area of Alex's wall

8 x 4 = 32

2. Area of Steve's wall

5 x 6 = 30

3. Alex's wall
4. 2 more blocks
5. 62

Page 212: Multiplication by Grouping

1. 3 x 3 = 9
2. 5 x 3 = 15
3. 6 x 3 = 18
4. 2 x 3 = 6
5. 4 x 3 = 12

Page 213: Mystery Message with Multiplication and Division

2. 102
3. 308
4. 62
5. 825
6. 231
7. 603
Answer: Herobrine

Page 214: Enderman's Guide to Place Value

2. E
3. F
4. A
5. C
6. G
7. D

Page 215: Skip Count Challenge

9, 18, 27, 36, 45, 54, 63, 72, 81, 90, 99, 108

Page 216: Telling Time

2. 7:55
3. 4:15
4. 9:20
5. 6:40
6. 12:05
7. 8:30
8. 5:10

Page 217: Spawn Egg Challenge

1. 135
2. 20
3. 188
4. 78
5. 40
6. 212
7. black
8. green and pink
9. 673

Pages 218-219: Equal Parts Challenge

1.
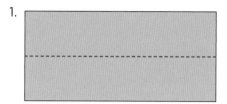

Fraction: $\frac{1}{2}$

2.
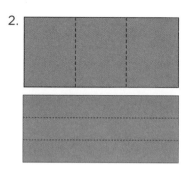

Fraction: $\frac{1}{3}$

3.
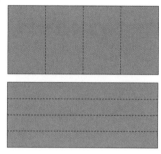

Fraction: $\frac{1}{4}$

Page 220: Mystery Message with Multiplication

2. 360
3. 243
4. 342
5. 246
6. 368
7. 336
8. 234
9. 350
10. 468
11. 328

Answer: Square Dancing

Page 221: Multiplication and Division Mystery Number

2. 48	3. 10	4. 7	5. 5	6. 4
7. 4	8. 5	9. 3	10. 7	

Page 22: Snow Golem's Number Challenge

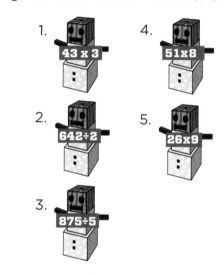

1. 43 x 3
2. 642 ÷ 2
3. 875 ÷ 5
4. 51 x 8
5. 26 x 9

Page 223: Skip Count Challenge

6, 12, 18, 24, 30, 36, 42, 48, 54, 60, 66, 72, 78, 84, 90

Pages 224-225: Creating Potions

1. 9, 9
2. 8, 20
3. 42, 54
4. 36, 63

Night Vision Potion	8	12	16	20
Fermented Spider Eyes	14	21	28	35

Pages 226-227: Adventures in Geometry: Perimeter and Area

1. Current perimeter: 26
   New perimeter: 34
2. Current perimeter: 22
   New perimeter: 16
3. Current perimeter: 18
   New perimeter: 26
4. Current area: 36
   New area: 72
5. Current area: 30
   New area: 15
6. Current area: 20
   New area: 40

Pages 228-229: Word Problems

1. 256 carrots
2. 144 seeds
3. 48 pearls
4. 64 baby zombies
5. 29 wheat items
6. 36 minutes
7. 34 trips
8. 126 wheat items

Page 230: Place Value

1. 180 (D)   2. 792 (G)
3. 405 (A)   4. 588 (E)
5. 576 (C)   6. 630 (B)
7. 208 (F)

Page 231: Ghastly Number Challenge

1. 24 x 38
2. 42 x 16
3. 44 x 7
4. 2200 ÷ 10
5. 76 x 10
6. 498 ÷ 2
7. 26 x 20

Pages 232-233: Mob Measurements

2. 30 inches
3. 37 inches
4. 51 inches
5. 18 inches

	Length in meters	Length in cm	Length in mm
	2	200	2,000
	4	400	4,000
	1.5	150	1,500
	2.5	250	2,500
	1	100	1,000

Pages 234-235: Adventures in Geometry

1. clock: obtuse
2. shovel: obtuse
3. ghast: acute
4. chicken: obtuse
5. inventory bar: right
6. potion: right
7. bow and arrow: acute
8. carrot: obtuse
9. pickaxe: acute

Page 236: Multiplication and Division Mystery Number

1. 7   2. 425   3. 137
4. 106   5. 8   6. 378
7. 8   8. 64   9. 78

Page 237: Mystery Message with Multiplication and Division

1. 446
2. 360
3. 89
4. 187
5. 819
6. 920
Answer: boxing

Page 238: Skeleton's Guide to Place Value

1. 131, Hundreds: 1
2. 51, Ones: 1
3. 491, Tens: 9
4. 14, Ones: 4
5. 85, Tens: 8
6. 501, Hundreds: 5
7. 267, Ones: 7

Page 239: Skip Count Challenge

96, 88, 80, 72, 64, 56, 48, 40, 32, 24, 16, 8

Pages 240-241: Animal Tally

1. 14 chickens
2. 56 chickens
3. 17 horses
4. 52 sheep
5. 49 cows
6. 7 cows

cow	7	49
pig	56	14
sheep	52	13
horse	17	51

Pages 242-243: Adventures in Geometry

1. bed: parallel
2. railway tracks: parallel
3. door: perpendicular
4. fish: intersecting
5. end crystal: intersecting
6. inventory bar: parallel
7. melon slice: parallel

Pages 244-245: Word Problems

1. 930 pickaxes
2. 210 legs
3. 13 carts
4. 300 flowers
5. 24 feet
6. 420 shulkers
7. 30 lily pads

Page 246: Giant's Guide to Place Value

1. 854, Tens: 5
2. 220, Hundreds: 2
3. 3,890, Thousands: 3
4. 7,047, Ones: 7
5. 80,065, Ten thousands: 8
6. 125, Hundreds: 1
7. 113,000, Hundred thousands: 1

Page 247: Skip Count Challenge

30, 60, 120, 240, 480, 960, 1,920, 3,840, 7,680, 15,360, 30,720, 61,440

Page 248: Comparing Fractions

1. 2/3 is greater, zombie wins
2. 7/8 is greater, wolf wins
3. 1/3 is greater, wolf wins
4. 6/20 is greater, zombie wins
5. 4/6 is greater, wolf wins
6. 4/8 is greater, wolf wins
7. 3/4 is greater, zombie wins
8. 5/6 is greater, wolf wins

Wolf won the most battles overall.

Page 249: Equal Fractions

		Minutes out of a half day (10 minutes)	Minutes out of a day (20 minutes)	Minutes out of a week (140 minutes)
farming		$^1/_{10}$	$^2/_{20}$	$^{14}/_{140}$
fighting		$^3/_{10}$	$^6/_{20}$	$^{42}/_{140}$
crafting		$^2/_{10}$	$^4/_{20}$	$^{28}/_{140}$
mining		$^4/_{10}$	$^8/_{20}$	$^{56}/_{140}$

Answer: Mining

Pages 250-251: Geometry Word Problems

1. 8 feet long
2. 9 bookcases
3. 30 feet wide
4. 192 feet
5. 768 emeralds
6. 8 feet wide
7. 6 feet long

MATH FOR MINECRAFTERS

Word Problems
grades 1 & 2

A NOTE TO PARENTS

When you want to reinforce classroom skills at home, it's crucial to have kid-friendly learning materials. This *Math for Minecrafters* workbook transforms math practice into an irresistible adventure complete with diamond swords, zombies, skeletons, and creepers. That means less arguing over homework and more fun overall.

Math for Minecrafters is also fully aligned with National Common Core Standards for 1st- and 2nd-grade math. What does that mean, exactly? All of the problems in this book correspond to what your child is expected to learn in school. This eliminates confusion and builds confidence for greater homework-time success!

As the workbook progresses, the word problems become more advanced. Encourage your child to progress at his or her own pace. Learning is best when students are challenged, but not frustrated. What's most important is that your Minecrafter is engaged in his or her own learning.

Whether it's the joy of seeing their favorite game characters on every page or the thrill of solving challenging problems just like Steve and Alex, there is something in this workbook to entice even the most reluctant math student.

Happy adventuring!

ADDING AND SUBTRACTING NUMBERS FROM 0 TO 10

Read the problem carefully. Use the pictures for extra help.
Write the answer in the space provided.

1. A skeleton shoots 7 arrows at you. Another skeleton shoots 2 arrows. How many arrows are shot at you?

2. You are attacked by 6 silverfish. You destroy 1 of them. How many silverfish are left?

3. A ghast shoots 10 fireballs at you. Only 2 of them hit you. How many fireballs miss you?

4. You spawn 10 creepers. You get out of the way as 3 of them blow up. How many creepers are left?

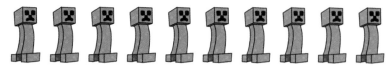

5. You find 7 shulkers in an End temple. You attack and destroy 4 of them. How many are left?

6. You place 3 torches on a cave wall but it's still really dark. You add 3 more torches to the wall. How many torches are on the wall?

7. You brew 4 potions of Strength and 2 potions of Night Vision. How many potions do you brew in all?

8. You start your game with 9 shovels in your inventory. You break 4 of them while digging. How many shovels do you have left?

ADDING AND SUBTRACTING NUMBERS FROM 0 TO 10

(continued from previous page)

9. You teleport 2 times in the morning and 2 times later in the day. How many times do you teleport?

10. You have 3 pieces of rotten flesh in your inventory. You attack zombies and get 4 more. How many pieces of rotten flesh do you have now?

11. You collect 8 gold ingots and use 2 of them to make a sword. How many gold ingots do you have left?

12. You find 6 chests in a cave and 4 more in another player's home. How many chests do you find in all?

13. You mine 10 blocks of obsidian. Then you use 3 of the blocks to build a tower. How many obsidian blocks do you have left?

14. You use 5 redstone ore blocks to build a wall. You use 5 more blocks to make the wall longer. How many redstone ore blocks do you use in all?

15. A group of 4 zombies attacks you in the night. Another group of 5 zombies attacks you later that night. How many zombies attack you in all?

HARDCORE MODE

Steve, Alex, and a villager collect as many purpur blocks as possible. Steve collects only 5 purpur blocks. The villager collects 4 more than Steve. Alex finds the most. She collects 3 more than the villager. How many purpur blocks does Alex collect?

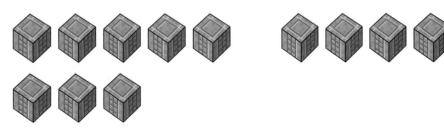

MATH RIDDLE CHALLENGE

Use your math smarts to fill in the answer to the riddle below:

Why don't zombies like running in races?

14 S 10 L 2 D 8 D 6 A 4 E 12 A 16 T

Count by **2's** to figure out the order of the letters above in the blank spaces below.

Because they always come in __ __ __ __ __ __ __ __ .

You've earned 10 math experience points!

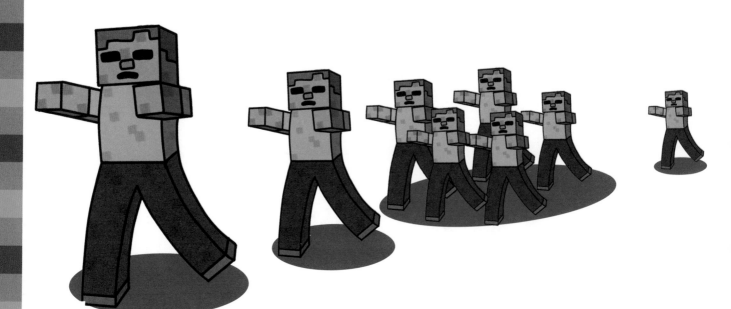

ADDING THREE NUMBERS FROM 0 TO 10

Read the problem carefully. Use the pictures for extra help.
Write the answer in the space provided.

1.  You build 2 towers, 2 beds, and 1 cobblestone house. How many things do you build in all?

2. You ride the rail cart for 3 minutes in the morning, 4 minutes in the afternoon, and 1 minute at night. How long do you ride the rail cart?

3. 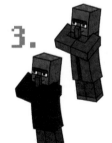 You trade 5 items with a blacksmith villager, 4 items with a priest villager, and 1 more item with a farmer villager. How many items do you trade in all?

4. You tame 1 wolf today, 2 wolves tomorrow, and 6 more wolves the next day. How many wolves do you tame in all?

ADDING THREE NUMBERS FROM 0 TO 10

(continued from previous page)

5. You fence in a group of 3 sheep. You bring 2 more sheep inside the fence. While the gate is open, 2 more sheep wander inside. How many sheep are fenced in now?

6. You get 5 experience points from every creeper you kill. You kill 2 creepers. How many experience points do you get?

7. You mine 7 blocks of redstone, 2 blocks of obsidian, and 1 block of granite. How many blocks do you mine in all?

8. You destroy 3 Endermen, 1 creeper, and 3 zombie pigmen. How many hostile mobs do you destroy?

9. A witch throws 6 potions of Poison, 3 potions of Slowness and 1 potion of Weakness. How many potions does the witch throw?

10. You see 5 Endermen when you enter the End, 2 more as you are fighting the Ender Dragon, and 1 more before you escape through the portal. How many Endermen do you see?

11. You tame 5 ocelots in the morning, 2 in the afternoon, and 2 more the next day. How many ocelots do you tame?

12. You discover 3 biomes in the Overworld, 1 in the Nether, and 1 in the End. How many biomes do you discover in all?

ADDING THREE NUMBERS FROM 0 TO 10

(continued from previous page)

13. You trade 3 emeralds to one villager and 3 more emeralds to the next villager you meet. You trade 1 more emerald to a third villager. How many emeralds do you trade in all?

14.  You craft 2 iron chest plates, 3 iron helmets, and 1 shield. How many pieces of armor do you craft in all?

15. A skeleton shoots 7 arrows at you, 1 at a villager, and 2 at an iron golem. How many arrows does he shoot in all?

HARDCORE MODE

There are 4 desert temples. Each one has 2 active traps. You deactivate 1 trap by breaking the pressure plate. How many active traps are left?

MATH RIDDLE CHALLENGE

Use your math smarts to fill in the answer to the riddle below:

What material do Minecrafters use to build their libraries?

Count by **4's** to figure out the order of the letters above in the blank spaces below.

__ __ __ __ - __ __ __ __ e **of course!**

You've earned 10 math experience points!

SUBTRACTING THREE NUMBERS FROM 0 TO 10

Read the problem carefully. Use the pictures for extra help.
Write the answer in the space provided.

1. You catch 10 fish with your fishing rod. You feed 3 to your cat and eat 2. How many fish are left?

2. There are 7 bats in a dungeon. You scare 2 away and destroy 1. How many bats are left?

3. 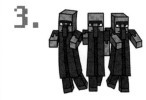 There are 6 villagers. During the night, 2 get turned into zombie villagers and wander away. One villager falls off a ledge. How many villagers are left?

4.  You have 8 diamond swords. You place 6 swords in a chest that gets blown up. You break 2 swords after using them for hours on end. How many diamond swords are left?

5. You get 10 skeleton spawn eggs in Creative mode. When used, 4 of them turn into wither skeletons and 1 burns up in the daylight. How many are left?

6. You find a wall made of 9 blocks of sandstone. You break 3 blocks with a wooden pickaxe, stop to rest, and then break 4 more blocks with a shovel. How many blocks of sandstone are left?

7. You have 7 diamonds. You use 3 to make diamond leggings and 2 to make a diamond sword. How many diamonds do you have left?

8. You have 8 blocks of wool in three colors: pink, lime, and yellow. 2 blocks are pink and 2 are yellow. How many blocks of lime wool do you have?

9. You approach a monster spawner in an Overworld dungeon. It spawns 6 monsters, including 2 spiders, 1 zombie, and some skeletons. How many skeletons are spawned?

10. You have 9 items in your inventory. 3 of them are food items, 2 are weapons, and the rest are building materials. How many items in your inventory are building materials?

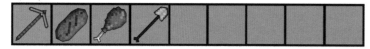

11. You battle the Ender Dragon a total of 10 times. You get destroyed by the Ender Dragon once and destroyed by Endermen twice. The rest of the times you win. How many times do you win?

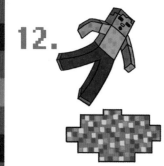

12. You battle 7 zombies near a lava pit. You use a Knockback enchantment to send 4 zombies flying backward into a lava pit. Then 2 zombies burn up in the daylight. How many zombies are left?

13. You start your game with 8 bones. You use 3 bones to make bone meal and 3 more to tame wolves. How many bones do you have left?

14. You battle 8 ghasts in the Nether. One ghast is destroyed when you deflect its fireballs and 3 more are destroyed by your arrows. How many ghasts are left?

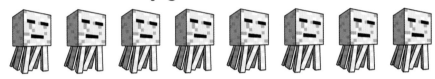

15. You start your game with 10 hearts. You fall off a hill and lose 3 hearts. You get hit by a zombie and lose 1 heart. How many hearts do you have left?

HARDCORE MODE

You craft 10 tools and 6 of them are shovels. The rest are equally divided between swords and pickaxes. How many swords and pickaxes did you craft?

MATH RIDDLE CHALLENGE

Use your math smarts to fill in the answer to the riddle below:

What did Alex say as she prepared to battle the skeleton horse?

30 T **10 B** **40 I** **5 A** **25 E** **15 O** **45 C** **35 P** **20 N**

Count by **5's** to figure out the order of the letters above in the blank spaces below.

I've got __ __ __ __ __   __ o __ __ __ k
with you!

You've earned 10 math experience points!

ADDING NUMBERS FROM 0 TO 20

Read the problem carefully. Use the pictures for extra help.
Write the answer in the space provided.

1. You are collecting Eyes of Ender to build an End portal. You get 6 Eyes of Ender from villagers and you craft 7 more. How many Eyes of Ender do you have in all?

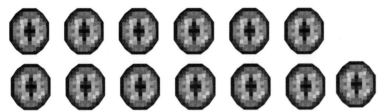

2. You make 10 bowls of mushroom stew and each bowl restores 2 hunger points. How many hunger points do you restore if you eat all of the mushroom stew?

3. You destroy a pair of snow golems. The first snow golem drops 8 snowballs, and the second snow golem drops 6. How many snowballs are dropped in all?

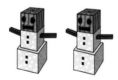

4. You craft 9 boats one week and 9 more boats the next week. How many boats do you craft in all?

5. There are 9 regular apples in your inventory and 7 golden apples. How many apples are in your inventory?

6. You catch 4 pufferfish to make a potion of Water Breathing. You catch 8 more pufferfish. How many pufferfish do you catch in all?

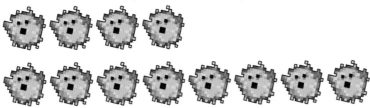

7. A polar bear drops 6 fish. Another polar bear drops 6 more fish. How many fish do both bears drop?

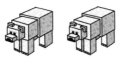

8. You craft 5 jack-o-lanterns in the morning and 7 jack-o-lanterns later in the day. How many jack-o-lanterns do you craft in all?

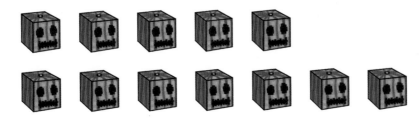

9. Your farm has 7 cows and 6 chickens. How many animals does your farm have in all?

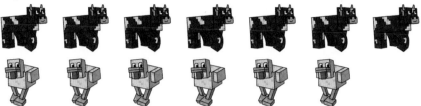

10.  You keep 7 pieces of armor in one chest and 8 pieces of armor in another. How many pieces of armor do you keep in all?

11. It takes you 14 minutes to craft a house and 6 minutes to craft a bed. How many minutes do you spend crafting both?

12. Your cobblestone house has 5 windows in the front and 6 windows in the back. How many windows does it have in all?

13. You fight 6 wither skeletons and 9 blazes in the Nether fortress. How many hostile mobs do you fight in all?

14. You place 8 grass blocks in a row. You place 8 more behind them. How many grass blocks do you place?

15.  You use your enchantment table to enchant 5 diamond swords and 6 iron shovels. How many items do you enchant in all?

HARDCORE MODE

If you encounter 6 wither skeletons and 3 blazes every time you enter the Nether fortress and you enter the Nether fortress 4 times, how many wither skeletons do you encounter in all?

MATH RIDDLE CHALLENGE

Use your math smarts to fill in the answer to the riddle below:

Why is it so easy to get around in the Overworld?

 18 L 36 K 42 W 24 O 12 B 30 C 48 Y 6 A

Count by **6's** to figure out the order of the letters above in the blank spaces below.

Because everything there is just __ __ __ __ __

a __ a __ .

You've earned 10 math experience points!

SUBTRACTING NUMBERS FROM 0 TO 20

Read the problem carefully. Use the pictures for extra help. Write the answer in the space provided.

1. You start a game with 14 hunger points and lose 7 hunger points after a long day of digging. How many hunger points do you have left?

2. You swing your sword at a zombie 12 times, but you only make contact 4 of those times. How many times do you swing your sword and miss?

3. You battle 13 creepers in the overworld. Your tamed wolf destroys 8 of them. How many are left for you to destroy?

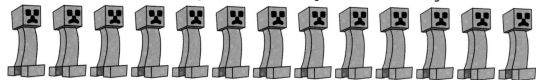

4. Squids drop 20 ink sacs into the water, but you are only able to collect 6 before you come up for air. How many ink sacs are still in the water?

5.  You have 17 minutes until nightfall and you spend 3 of those minutes crafting a bed. How many minutes are left until nightfall?

6. You have 13 empty buckets. You fill 6 of them with milk. How many empty buckets are left?

7. You meet 20 ocelots in the jungle biome. You tame 4 of them and they follow you home. How many ocelots are left untamed?

8.  You have 17 blocks, but you only need 9 blocks to build a beacon. How many blocks do you have left over after you build your beacon?

SUBTRACTING NUMBERS FROM 0 TO 20

(continued from previous page)

9. You are attacked by 12 spiders, but you kill 5 of them. How many spiders are left?

10. Creepers drop 14 units of gunpowder. You collect 9 of them. How many units of gunpowder are left?

11. You find 16 cobwebs in an abandoned mineshaft. You use your shears to collect 3 of them. How many cobwebs are left?

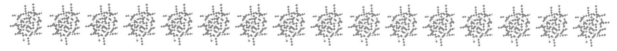

12. Zombie pigmen attack a village where 19 villagers live. When you arrive at the village, only 4 villagers have survived. How many villagers were destroyed in the attack?

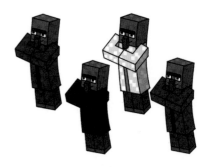

13. A ghast hurls 11 fireballs at you. You are hit by 5 of them. How many fireballs miss you?

14. You have 16 spawn eggs in your inventory. You use 3 of them. How many spawn eggs do you have left?

15. You are trying to build an 18-step staircase out of wood blocks. You build 9 steps and stop to eat. How many more steps do you need to build?

HARDCORE MODE

If each of the Wither's 3 heads spits 8 skulls at you during a battle, and 14 out of all the skulls miss you, how many skulls hit you?

MATH RIDDLE CHALLENGE

Use your math smarts to fill in the answer to the riddle below:

Why does Steve hate driving places?

28 D 35 B 14 R 56 K 7 A 42 L 21 O 49 C

Count by **7's** to figure out the order of the letters above in the blank spaces below.

Because he's always hitting

__ __ __a __   __ __o __ __.

You've earned 10 math experience points!

ADDING AND SUBTRACTING NUMBERS FROM 0 TO 20

Read the problem carefully. Use the pictures for extra help.
Write the answer in the space provided.

1. 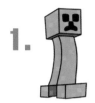 You put down 14 minecart rails and a creeper blows up 6 of them. How many rails are left?

2.  You transport 15 chests to your base using your new railway system. You transport 5 more. How many chests do you transport in all?

3. You visit the desert biome 12 times and the jungle biome 7 times. How many more times do you visit the desert biome?

4. A group of 15 zombie villagers are headed your way. You only have enough splash potion and golden apples to turn 7 of them back into villagers. How many will remain zombies?

ADDING AND SUBTRACTING NUMBERS FROM 0 TO 20

(continued from previous page)

5. You ride 6 pigs and 12 horses with your new leather saddle. How many animals do you ride in all?

6.  You come across a herd of 16 mooshrooms grazing in the mushroom island biome. You count 8 baby mooshrooms, but the rest are adults. How many adult mooshrooms are in the herd?

7. You drink 4 potions of Water Breathing and 9 potions of Strength. How many potions do you drink in all?

8. You visit the End 11 times, but only find elytra 4 of those times. How many times do you visit the End and not find elytra?

9. An iron golem drops 13 red flowers. You collect 6 of them. How many flowers are left?

10. You want to mine 17 layers of diamond ore. You mine 4 layers. How many layers are left to mine?

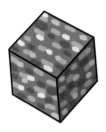

11. You dig through 12 layers of lapis lazuli ore and rest. You dig through 6 more. How many layers of lapis lazuli ore do you dig through?

12. You need 20 iron blocks to build a small shelter. You only have 3 of them. How many more blocks do you need?

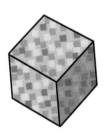

ADDING AND SUBTRACTING NUMBERS FROM 0 TO 20

(continued from previous page)

13. 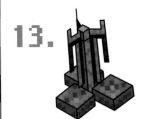 You need 11 ingredients to make a potion. You only have 4 of the ingredients. How many more ingredients do you need?

14. You chop down a total of 13 trees. You eat to restore your hunger points and then chop down 5 more. How many trees do you chop in all?

15. You climb 11 steps of stairs on your way to collect some diamonds. You climb 7 more steps. How many steps do you climb in all?

HARDCORE MODE

It takes 6 bites for a player to finish eating a cake. How many bites does it take for a player to eat 3 and a half cakes?

MATH RIDDLE CHALLENGE

Use your math smarts to fill in the answer to the riddle below:

What does Steve tell himself before he steps bravely through the portal?

40	16	8	32	64	24	48	56
E	N	I	H	D	T	E	N

Count by **8's** to figure out the order of the letters above in the blank spaces below.

"It will all work out __ __   __ __ __   __ __ __.**"**

You've earned 10 math experience points!

ADDING THREE NUMBERS FROM 0 TO 20

Read the problem carefully. Use the pictures for extra help.
Write the answer in the space provided.

1. You craft 1 brewing stand, 15 pressure plates, and 4 firework rockets. How many items do you craft in all?

2. You destroy 5 hostile mobs, 6 neutral mobs, and 2 boss mobs. How many mobs do you destroy?

3. You build a tower with 7 clay blocks, 4 granite blocks, and 6 gravel blocks. How many blocks do you use to build your tower?

4. While you're playing, 3 herds of cows spawn. One herd has 7 cows, another herd has 5 cows, and the last herd has 6 cows. How many cows spawn in all?

5. Zombies spawn in groups of 4. While you're playing, 3 groups of zombies spawn in the Overworld. How many zombies spawn in all?

6. You trade 12 emeralds to the first villager you see, 2 emeralds to the next villager, and 3 more to the next villager. How many emeralds do you trade in all?

7.  You build 9 beacons your first day, 2 beacons the next day, and 3 beacons the third day. How many beacons do you build in all?

8. You place 5 minecart rails in the morning, 7 in the afternoon, and 7 more later that night. How many minecart rails do you place in all?

ADDING THREE NUMBERS FROM 0 TO 20

(continued from previous page)

9. You battle 9 skeletons, 4 zombies, and 3 creepers in one day of gaming. How many mobs do you battle in all?

10. You enchant 3 books, 8 swords, and 2 pieces of armor. How many items do you enchant in all?

11. You shoot 7 arrows at a creeper, 8 at a skeleton, and 4 at a giant zombie. How many arrows do you shoot in all?

12. You survive 2 creeper explosions at your spawn point, 5 more near your farm, and 5 more inside your shelter. How many creeper explosions do you survive?

13.  A witch throws 1 potion of Slowness, 3 potions of Weakness, and 8 potions of Poison. How many potions does the witch throw in all?

14. You tame 6 wolves, 3 horses, and 7 ocelots. How many animals do you tame in all?

15. The Ender Dragon fires 6 Ender charges at you when it first circles you, 6 more as it circles the second time, and 7 more before you succeed in defeating it. How many Ender charges does the Ender Dragon fire in all?

HARDCORE MODE

You battle 8 ghasts and take a little damage. You battle two more pairs of ghasts and take more damage. How many ghasts do you battle in all?

MATH RIDDLE CHALLENGE

Use your math smarts to fill in the answer to the riddle below:

Why doesn't anyone want to play with the Ender Dragon or the Wither?

45 O   9 T   63 S   18 O   72 Y   54 S   36 B   27 O

Count by **9's** to figure out the order of the letters above in the blank spaces below.

Because they're __ __ __   __ __ __ __- __ !

You've earned 10 math experience points!

SUBTRACTION WITH THREE NUMBERS FROM 0 TO 20

Read the problem carefully. Use the pictures for extra help.
Write the answer in the space provided.

1. You start with 18 experience points, but you use 4 of those points enchanting a bow and arrow and 1 point enchanting a book. How many experience points do you have left?

2. You place 14 lily pads on water blocks to cross a river, but 6 of them are destroyed by a boat and 3 more are caught by a fisherman villager. How many lily pads are left?

3. A stack of three cacti is 19 blocks tall. One cactus is 5 blocks tall and another cactus is 4 blocks tall. How many blocks tall is the third cactus?

4. You place 15 items in your chest. You know that 3 of them are diamonds and 5 of them are enchanted books. The rest are gunpowder. How many items of gunpowder do you have in your chest?

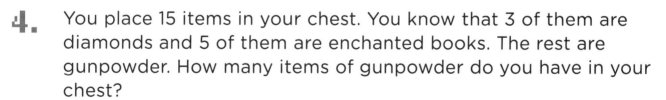

SUBTRACTION WITH THREE NUMBERS FROM 0 TO 20

(continued from previous page)

5. You meet 15 villagers in one day. Of those villagers, 4 are blacksmith villagers and 1 is a priest villager. The rest of the villagers are librarians. How many of the villagers are librarians?

6. There are 12 snow golems. Of those snow golems, 2 melt in a sudden rainstorm and 3 melt in the jungle biome. How many snow golems are left?

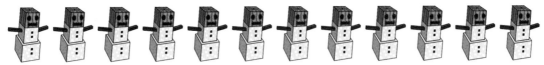

7. You chop down 13 trees. 6 of them are oak trees, 3 of them are birch trees, and the rest are spruce trees. How many trees are spruce trees?

8. You collect 20 Ender pearls after battling a group of Endermen. You use 4 of those Ender pearls to make an Eye of Ender. You lose 2 of them when a mob steals your treasure chest. How many Ender pearls do you still have?

9.  You have 17 lumps of coal in your inventory. You burn 12 in your furnace and trade 4 to villagers. How many lumps of coal do you have left?

10.  You have 11 zombie eggs in your inventory. You spawn zombies from 5 of the eggs and baby zombies from 3 of the eggs. The rest of the eggs are still in your inventory. How many zombie eggs are still in your inventory?

11. You are down to 0 hunger points. You get 14 hunger points from eating cookies. You lose 5 hunger points while battling, and lose 5 more hunger points while mining. How many hunger points do you have left?

12. You brew 13 potions of Weakness. You use 6 potions (plus some golden apples) to heal zombie villagers and 2 to weaken skeletons during a battle. How many potions of Weakness do you have left?

SUBTRACTION WITH THREE NUMBERS FROM 0 TO 20

(continued from previous page)

13. Your first full day of Minecrafting lasts for 20 minutes. You spend 9 minutes searching for resources and 3 minutes building structures. How many minutes do you have until the day ends?

14. You have 19 wood planks. You use 4 to make a boat and 3 to make a bed. How many wood planks do you have left?

15. You see 14 donkeys in the plains biome. In the next few minutes, 6 of them wander away and 2 are blown up by a creeper. How many donkeys are left?

HARDCORE MODE

Your mom gives you 30 minutes of gaming time. You spend up 8 of those minutes trying to remember your password, so you ask your mom for more gaming time. Your mom lets you add 4 minutes to your gaming time. How much gaming time do you have now?

MATH RIDDLE CHALLENGE

Use your math smarts to fill in the answer to the riddle below:

What does an Enderman pack when he goes on vacation?

90 A 30 A 10 C 80 E 60 E 40 E 100 R 20 E 50 N 70 R

Count by **10's** to figure out the order of the letters above in the blank spaces below.

He packs lots of   __ l __ __ n   __ __ d __ __- w __ __ __!

You've earned 10 math experience points!

ADDING AND SUBTRACTING THREE OR FOUR NUMBERS FROM 0 TO 20

Read the problem carefully. Use the pictures for extra help. Write the answer in the space provided.

1. You are attacked by a group of 16 Endermen. You destroy 2 of them with your sword. You scare 6 Endermen away with water. How many Endermen are still attacking?

2. You battle a group of 5 ghasts in the Nether. Each ghast shoots 2 fireballs at you. You deflect 3 of the fireballs, but the rest of the them hit you and destroy you. How many fireballs hit you?

3.  You build 5 cobblestone structures, 7 wood structures, and 4 obsidian structures. How many structures do you build in all?

4. You want to cure 12 zombie villagers, but you only have enough golden apples to cure 4 of them. You craft a few more golden apples and cure 3 more zombie villagers. How many villagers are still zombies?

5. A group of 20 zombies approach a village. An iron golem attacks and destroys 6 of the zombies. You destroy 3 of the zombies. How many zombies are left?

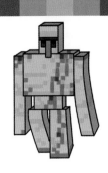

6.  You craft 11 iron swords, 4 golden swords, and 3 chest plates. After many battles, 6 of the iron swords break. How many swords are left?

7. 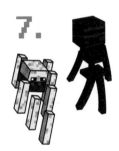 You craft a brewing stand and use it to brew 14 potions. You use 5 potions on a blaze, 1 on a wither skeleton, and 2 on zombie pigmen. How many potions are left?

8. You craft 17 items. Of those, 5 of them are swords. The rest are an equal amount of chest plates and helmets. How many chest plates and helmets do you craft?

ADDING AND SUBTRACTING THREE OR FOUR NUMBERS FROM 0 TO 20

(continued from previous page)

9. There are 14 hostile mobs that walk into lava blocks. If 6 of the hostile mobs are zombie pigmen (which are immune to fire), 3 are ghasts (also immune to fire), and the rest take damage, how many hostile mobs take damage?

10. You collect 9 gold ingots one day, 5 the next, and 10 the next. You use 4 of them to make a clock. How many gold ingots do you have left?

11. You make 6 wooden hoes one day and 3 the next. It takes 2 wooden sticks to make a wooden hoe. How many sticks did you use to make all of the wooden hoes?

12.  You face the Wither 17 times in one week. You escape 3 times and are destroyed 12 times. The rest of the times, you defeat the Wither. How many times do you defeat the Wither?

13.  You need 20 diamonds to make full diamond armor. You mine 7 from diamond ore and you collect 4 more from a chest. How many more diamonds do you need to make full armor?

14.  You teleport 8 times in the morning and 7 times in the afternoon. If you teleport 18 times total that day, how many more times do you teleport?

15. You catch 4 fish in the morning, 16 fish later that day, and 2 more in the evening. You use 7 of your fish to tame ocelots. How many fish are left?

HARDCORE MODE

Write your own addition or subtraction problem below and show it to your friend, your teacher, or your parent. Challenge them to solve it!

_____

_____

_____

_____

MATH RIDDLE CHALLENGE

Use your math smarts to fill in the answer to the riddle below:

Why did Steve place a chicken on top of a shining tower?

 110 S   88 G   55 O   44 C   11 B   33 A   77 E   66 N   22 E   99 G

Count by **11's** to figure out the order of the letters above in the blank spaces below.

He wanted to make   __ __ __ __ __ __   and   __ __ __ __!

You've earned 10 math experience points!

ADDING NUMBERS FROM 0 TO 100

Read the problem carefully. Use the pictures for extra help. Write the answer in the space provided.

1. You spawn 26 husks in the desert biome and 13 baby husks. How many husks do you spawn in all?

2. You stack 24 blocks of glowstone on top of 33 blocks of gold ore. How many blocks are stacked in all?

3. You see 18 spiders while exploring a cave and 11 more on your way back to your shelter. How many spiders do you see in all?

4. You catch 14 pufferfish on your first day fishing and 67 regular fish the second day. How many fish do you catch in all?

ADDING NUMBERS FROM 0 TO 100

(continued from previous page)

5. You are attacked by 22 slimes one night and 37 slimes another night. How many slimes attack you in all?

6. You and your tamed wolf battle a group of endermites. Your wolf destroys 15 and you destroy 63. How many endermites do you destroy in all?

7. You eat 45 cookies to gain hunger points. You eat 12 mushroom stew to gain more hunger points. How many food items do you eat in all?

8. In the course of a day, you battle a lot of witches. They drop 13 spider eyes and 22 glass bottles. How many items do the witches drop in all?

9. You craft a house using 17 wood blocks and 72 cobblestone blocks. How many blocks do you use in all?

10. You spawn 51 creepers on your mob farm one day and 33 creepers the next day. How many creepers do you spawn in all?

11.  You destroy a group of chickens and collect 62 feathers. You destroy more chickens and collect 18 feathers. How many feathers do you collect in all?

12. You add 43 iron ore to your inventory and 15 golden ore. You already had 4 redstone ore in your inventory. How many pieces of ore do you have in all?

ADDING NUMBERS FROM 0 TO 100

(continued from previous page)

13.  You meet 14 polar bears in the ice plains biome and 22 rabbits. How many animals do you meet in all?

14. You grow 11 flowers one day and 44 flowers the next. How many flowers do you grow in all?

15.  You fly over 10 blocks wearing your elytra. You swoop down and fly over 12 more blocks. How many blocks do you fly over in all?

HARDCORE MODE

A charged creeper explodes near a mob of zombies and 16 zombie heads are dropped. You collect half of them. If you add them to the 61 zombie heads in your inventory, how many zombie heads do you have in all?

MATH RIDDLE CHALLENGE

Use your math smarts to fill in the answer to the riddle below:

Why doesn't Alex remember what she reads?

84 E 108 N 72 T 36 P 12 S 48 S 24 K 60 O 96 E

Count by **12's** to figure out the order of the letters above in the blank spaces below.

Because she always __ __ i __ __   t __   __ h _   __ __ d !

You've earned 10 math experience points!

SUBTRACTING NUMBERS FROM 0 TO 100

Read the problem carefully. Use the pictures for extra help. Write the answer in the space provided.

1. You are attacked by 44 Endermen in the End. You place water buckets nearby and 12 of the Endermen teleport away. How many Endermen are left?

2. You have 32 saplings. Of those, 25 of them are birch saplings and the rest are oak saplings. How many are oak saplings?

3. You have a total of 51 books in your inventory. Only 6 of them are enchanted. How many books in your inventory are not enchanted?

4. You fight a group of 68 silverfish and destroy 11 of them. How many silverfish are left?

5.  You destroy 48 skeletons, but only 11 of them drop arrows. The rest drop bones. How many drop bones?

6.  You enter the Nether and 34 zombie pigmen attack you. You destroy 27 of the zombie pigmen. How many are left?

7. You have 23 enchantment levels. You spend 14 enchanting your sword. How many enchantment levels do you have left?

8. You make 67 pieces of gold armor. Of those, 43 of them are chest plates. How many are not chest plates?

SUBTRACTING NUMBERS FROM 0 TO 100

(continued from previous page)

9.  A creeper explodes 88 times a day. Half of those explosions cause damage to a mob. The rest of the explosions cause damage to a player. How many of the explosions cause damage to a player?

10. A zombie is 67 blocks away from you. He walks 52 blocks closer. How many blocks are between you and the zombie?

11. You enjoy 60 minutes of Minecrafting after school. You spend 40 of those minutes playing survival mode and the rest playing creative mode. How many minutes do you spend in creative mode?

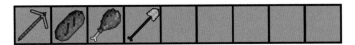

HARDCORE MODE

You have 12 lapis lazuli ore blocks, 36 gold ore blocks, 25 lava blocks, and 60 ice blocks. How many blocks do you have in all?

MATH RIDDLE CHALLENGE

Use your math smarts to fill in the answer to the riddle below:

What is a ghast's favorite dessert?

 135 M   90 R   60 S   30 C   105 E   15 I   45 E   75 C 120 A

Count by **15's** to figure out the order of the letters above in the blank spaces below.

— — —   — — — — — —

You've earned 10 math experience points!

ADDITION AND SUBTRACTION WITH REGROUPING

1.  You meet 52 wolves in the Overworld. You tame 18 of them. How many wolves are still untamed?

2.  You destroy 88 hostile mobs in one day. The next day you destroy 16 more. How many hostile mobs do you destroy in all?

3. 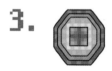 You earn 73 experience orbs in one day of gaming. You lose 36 of them when you come into contact with lava. How many experience orbs do you have left?

4.  You travel a distance of 43 blocks in your minecart. If you travel backward 15 blocks, how far are you from where you started?

5. You have 92 spawn eggs in your inventory. You discover that 17 of them are creeper eggs. How many are not creeper eggs?

6.  You see a herd of 64 cows. You feed them wheat and 18 baby cows appear. How many cows are there now?

7.  You harvest 25 wheat one day and 36 wheat the next day. How many wheat do you harvest in all?

8.  One creeper explosion leaves a hole 49 blocks long. Another creeper leaves a hole next to it that's 68 blocks long. How many blocks long are both holes combined?

CONGRATULATIONS

YOU'VE EARNED

THE POTION OF MATH ABILITY!

This potion gives you the ability
to tackle math challenges of all kinds.

Count up your experience points from the Math Riddle Challenge
pages and write the total below:

It's time to upgrade to a new experience level.
Try *Math for Minecrafters, Word Problems Grades 3 & 4* next!

ANSWER KEY

PAGE 260

1. 9 arrows
2. 5 silverfish
3. 8 fireballs
4. 7 creepers

PAGE 261

5. 3 shulkers
6. 6 torches
7. 6 potions
8. 5 shovels

PAGE 262

9. 4 times
10. 7 pieces
11. 6 gold ingots
12. 10 chests

PAGE 263

13. 7 obsidian blocks
14. 10 redstone ore blocks
15. 9 zombies

Hardcore mode
12 purpur blocks

PAGE 264

Why don't zombies like running in races?
Because they always come in dead last.

PAGE 265

1. 5 things
2. 8 minutes
3. 10 items
4. 9 wolves

PAGE 266

5. 7 sheep
6. 10 experience points
7. 10 blocks
8. 7 hostile mobs

PAGE 267

9. 10 potions
10. 8 Endermen
11. 9 ocelots
12. 5 biomes

PAGE 268

13. 7 emeralds
14. 6 pieces of armor
15. 10 arrows

Hardcore mode
7 active traps

PAGE 269

What are all Minecrafters libraries built from?
Read-stone of course!

PAGE 270

1. 5 fish
2. 4 bats
3. 3 villagers
4. 0 diamond swords

PAGE 271

5. 5 skeleton spawn eggs
6. 2 blocks of sandstone
7. 2 diamonds
8. 4 blocks of lime wool

PAGE 272

9. 3 skeletons
10. 4 building materials
11. 7 times
12. 1 zombie

PAGE 273

13. 2 bones
14. 4 ghasts
15. 6 hearts

Hardcore mode
2 swords, 2 pickaxes

PAGE 274

What did Alex say as she prepared to battle the skeleton horse?

I've got a bone to pick with you!

PAGE 275

1. 13 Eyes of Ender
2. 20 hunger points
3. 14 snowballs
4. 18 boats

PAGE 276

5. 16 apples
6. 12 pufferfish
7. 12 fish
8. 12 jack-o-lanterns

PAGE 277

9. 13 animals
10. 15 pieces of armor
11. 20 minutes
12. 11 windows

PAGE 278

13. 15 hostile mobs
14. 16 grass blocks
15. 11 items

Hardcore mode
24 wither skeletons

PAGE 279

Why is it so easy to get around in the Overworld?
Because everything there is just a block away.

PAGE 280

1. 7 hunger points
2. 8 swings
3. 5 creepers
4. 14 ink sacs

PAGE 281

5. 14 minutes
6. 7 empty buckets
7. 16 ocelots
8. 8 blocks

PAGE 282

9. 7 spiders
10. 5 units
11. 13 cobwebs
12. 15 villagers

PAGE 283

13. 6 fireballs
14. 13 spawn eggs
15. 9 more steps

Hardcore mode
10 skulls

PAGE 284

Why does Steve hate driving places?
Because he's always hitting a road block.

PAGE 285

1. 8 rails
2. 20 chests
3. 5 more times
4. 8 villagers

PAGE 286

5. 18 animals
6. 8 adult mooshrooms
7. 13 potions
8. 7 times

PAGE 287

9. 7 flowers
10. 13 layers
11. 18 layers
12. 17 blocks

PAGE 288

13. 7 ingredients
14. 18 trees
15. 18 steps

Hardcore mode
21 bites

PAGE 289

What does Steve tell himself before he steps bravely through the portal?
"It will all work out in the End."

PAGE 290

1. 20 items
2. 13 mobs
3. 17 blocks
4. 18 cows

PAGE 291

5. 12 zombies
6. 17 emeralds
7. 14 beacons
8. 19 minecart rails

PAGE 292

9. 16 mobs
10. 13 items
11. 19 arrows
12. 12 explosions

PAGE 293

13. 12 potions
14. 16 animals
15. 19 Ender charges

Hardcore mode
12 ghasts

PAGE 294

Why doesn't anyone want to play with the Ender Dragon or the Wither?
Because they're too boss-y!
(Get it? They're boss mobs!)

PAGE 295

1. 13 experience points
2. 5 lily pads
3. 10 blocks
4. 7 units of gunpowder

PAGE 296

5. 10 villagers
6. 7 snow golems
7. 4 spruce trees
8. 14 Ender pearls

PAGE 297

9. 1 lump of coal
10. 3 zombie eggs
11. 4 hunger points
12. 5 potions of Weakness

PAGE 298

13. 8 minutes
14. 12 wood planks
15. 6 donkeys

Hardcore mode
26 minutes of gaming time

PAGE 299

What does an Enderman pack when he goes on vacation?
He packs lots of clean Ender-wear!

PAGE 300

1. 8 Endermen
2. 7 fireballs
3. 16 structures
4. 5 villagers

PAGE 301

5. 11 zombies
6. 9 swords
7. 6 potions
8. 6 chest plates and 6 helmets

PAGE 302

9. 5 hostile mobs
10. 20 gold ingots
11. 18 sticks
12. 2 times

PAGE 303

13. 9 diamonds
14. 3 times
15. 15 fish

PAGE 304

Why did Steve place a chicken on top of a shining tower?
He wanted to make beacon and eggs!

PAGE 305

1. 39 husks
2. 57 blocks
3. 29 spiders
4. 81 fish

PAGE 306

5. 59 slimes
6. 78 endermites
7. 57 food items
8. 35 items

PAGE 307

9. 89 blocks
10. 84 creepers
11. 80 feathers
12. 62 ore

PAGE 308

13. 36 animals
14. 55 flowers
15. 22 blocks

Hardcore mode
69 zombie heads

PAGE 309

Why doesn't Alex remember what she reads?
Because she always skips to the End!

PAGE 310

1. 32 endermen
2. 7 saplings
3. 45 books
4. 57 silverfish

PAGE 311

5. 37 skeletons
6. 7 zombie pigmen
7. 9 enchantment levels
8. 24 pieces of armor

PAGE 312

9. 44 explosions
10. 15 blocks
11. 20 minutes

Hardcore mode
133 blocks

PAGE 313

What is a ghast's favorite dessert?
ice scream

PAGE 314

1. 34 wolves
2. 104 hostile mobs
3. 37 experience orbs
4. 28 blocks

PAGE 315

5. 75 eggs
6. 82 cows
7. 61 wheat
8. 117 blocks long

MATH FOR MINECRAFTERS

Word Problems

grades 3 & 4

A NOTE TO PARENTS

When you want to reinforce classroom skills at home, it's crucial to have kid-friendly learning materials. This *Math for Minecrafters* workbook transforms math practice into an irresistible adventure complete with diamond swords, zombies, skeletons, and creepers. That means less arguing over homework and more fun overall.

Math for Minecrafters is also fully aligned with National Common Core Standards for 3rd- and 4th-grade math. What does that mean, exactly? All of the problems in this book correspond to what your child is expected to learn in school. This eliminates confusion and builds confidence for greater homework-time success!

As the workbook progresses, the word problems become more advanced. Encourage your child to progress at his or her own pace. Learning is best when students are challenged, but not frustrated. What's most important is that your Minecrafter is engaged in his or her own learning.

Whether it's the joy of seeing their favorite game characters on every page or the thrill of solving challenging problems just like Steve and Alex, there is something in this workbook to entice even the most reluctant math student.

Happy adventuring!

MULTIPLYING ONE-DIGIT NUMBERS

Read the problem carefully. Use the pictures for extra help. Write the answer in the space provided.

1. You meet 8 skeletons and each one shoots 7 arrows at you. How many arrows are shot in all?

2. You are attacked by 6 groups of 4 silverfish. How many silverfish are attacking in all?

3. A ghast shoots 10 fireballs at you. A group of 3 more ghasts approaches and each ghast shoots 2 fireballs at you. How many fireballs are shot at you in all?

4.  You see 10 creepers. You get 3 unit of gunpowder from each of them. How many unit of gunpowder do you get in all?

5. You find 7 shulkers in an End temple. You take 4 damage from each of them. How much damage do you take in all?

6. You place 3 torches on each of 3 cave walls. How many torches do you place?

7. You brew 4 potions of Leaping and each one restores 2 hearts. How many hearts can be restored with 8 potions of Leaping?

8. You start your game with 9 shovels in your inventory. You have 3 times as many swords in your inventory. How many swords do you have?

MULTIPLYING ONE-DIGIT NUMBERS

(continued from previous page)

9. You encounter 6 groups of 7 cave spiders. How many spiders do you encounter?

10. You destroy a bunch of zombies and collect 5 pieces of rotten flesh. If you collect this much rotten flesh 3 times in one day, how many pieces of rotten flesh do you collect in all?

11. To make one golden sword, you need 2 gold ingots. If you want to make 8 golden swords, how many gold ingots do you need?

12. You find 7 chests in each of 3 caves that you explore. How many chests do you find in all?

13. You make 3 towers. Each one is made of 10 blocks of obsidian. How many obsidian blocks do you use in all?

14. You stack 4 rows of 5 redstone ore blocks to build a wall. How many redstone ore blocks do you use in all?

15. A group of 4 skeletons attacks you. Each skeleton shoots 8 arrows at you. How many arrows do the skeletons shoot in all?

HARDCORE MODE

Steve, Alex, and a villager collect as many emeralds as possible. Steve only collects 3 emeralds. The villager collects 4 times as many emeralds as Steve. Alex collects the most. She collects 6 times as many emeralds as the villager.

How many emeralds does Alex collect?

PVP SHOWDOWN

Which player earned the most experience points today? Solve the equations in each column then add up the answers to determine the winner of this PVP showdown.

1.　7 x 6 =　　　　6 x 8 =

2.　3 x 5 =　　　　4 x 9 =

3.　8 x 4 =　　　　6 x 2 =

4.　9 x 1 =　　　　3 x 3 =

5.　4 x 7 =　　　　9 x 6 =

6.　6 x 6 =　　　　3 x 8 =

TOTAL POINTS　　_____　　　_____

Circle the winner:

 ALEX　　　 STEVE

MULTIPLYING ONE- AND TWO-DIGIT NUMBERS

Read the problem carefully. Use the pictures for extra help. Write the answer in the space provided.

1.  You use 20 blocks of cobblestone to build a tower. How many blocks of cobblestone do you use to build 4 towers?

2. A player rides in the railcart 15 times a day. After 3 days, how many times does the player ride in the railcart?

3. There are 14 blacksmith villagers who have 3 emeralds each. How many emeralds do the Blacksmith villagers have in all?

4.

You tame 2 wolves a day for 16 days. How many wolves do you tame in all?

MULTIPLYING ONE- AND TWO-DIGIT NUMBERS

(continued from previous page)

5. You have 4 farms with 17 sheep on each farm. How many sheep do you have in all?

6. You get 11 experience points from every creeper you kill. You kill 4 creepers. How many experience points do you get?

7. You mine 8 blocks of granite for 16 mornings straight. How many blocks do you mine in all?

8. You destroy 3 times more Endermen than zombie pigmen. You destroy 25 zombie pigmen. How many Endermen do you destroy?

9. Seven witches throw 26 splash potions in a day. How many splash potions do the witches throw in all?

10. 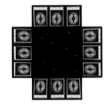 You see 4 groups of 16 Endermen when you enter the End. How many Endermen do you see in all?

11. You tame 5 ocelots every time you enter the Jungle Biome. You enter the Jungle Biome 32 times. How many ocelots do you tame?

12.  You use a map 8 times every time you play. If you play 22 times, how many times do you use a map?

MULTIPLYING ONE- AND TWO-DIGIT NUMBERS

(continued from previous page)

13. You need 3 lapis lazuli to craft each enchanted bow and arrow. How many lapis lazuli do you need to make 19 enchanted bow and arrows?

14.  You destroy 15 ghasts in 8 minutes. If you continue at that rate, how many ghasts will you destroy in 24 minutes?

15.  A skeleton shoots 7 arrows at each villager he sees. He sees 29 villagers. How many arrows does he shoot?

HARDCORE MODE

There are 14 desert temples. Each one has 10 active traps. You deactivate 14 of the traps by breaking the pressure plate. How many active traps are left?

PVP SHOWDOWN

Which player earned the most experience points today? Solve the equations in each column then add up the answers to determine the winner of this PVP showdown.

1.	12 x 6 =	10 x 8 =
2.	3 x 50 =	14 x 9 =
3.	11 x 4 =	16 x 2 =
4.	19 x 1 =	3 x 13 =
5.	24 x 2 =	15 x 6 =
6.	6 x 13 =	12 x 8 =
TOTAL POINTS	_____	_____

Circle the winner:

 ALEX   STEVE

DIVISION WITH 1- AND 2-DIGIT NUMBERS

Read the problem carefully. Use the pictures for extra help. Write the answer in the space provided.

1. You catch 9 fish with your fishing rod. You divide the fish among 3 cats. How many fish does each cat get?

2. There are 8 bats in 4 dungeons. If each dungeon has the same number of bats, how many bats are in each one?

3. There are 6 villagers. If each house in the village can fit 3 villagers, how many houses do they need?

4.  You have 4 diamond swords. You store 1 sword in each chest you own. How many chests do you own?

5. You have 15 skeleton spawn eggs. You sort them into 5 equal groups. How many eggs are in each group?

6. You make 3 identical walls out of 12 blocks of sandstone. How many blocks of sandstone do you use for each wall?

7. You have 18 diamonds. You give 6 of them to each villager you see until you're all out of diamonds. How many villagers did you see?

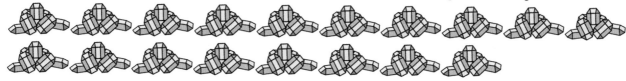

8. You have 16 blocks of wool in 4 different colors: blue, pink, lime, and yellow. If you have the same amount of every color, how many blocks do you have in each color?

9.  You approach a monster spawner in an Overworld dungeon. It spawns 20 monsters in all. If it spawns 5 of each kind of monster, how many kinds of monsters does it spawn?

10. You have 12 Ender eye pearls in your inventory. You place an equal amount in two different chests. How many Ender eye pearls do you place in each chest?

11. You battle the Ender Dragon a total of 16 times. Half of those times, you win. How many times do you win?

12.  You earn 24 experience orbs for destroying a group of zombies. If every zombie you destroy earns you 6 experience orbs, how many zombies did you destroy?

13. You start your game with 20 bones. You need 2 bones to tame every wolf. How many wolves can you tame?

14. You battle 24 ghasts in the Nether. If you destroy 3 ghasts a minute, how many minutes does it take to destroy all of the ghasts?

15. A player has 10 hearts. He loses 1 heart every time he runs into a zombie. How many zombies can he run into before he's out of hearts?

HARDCORE MODE

You craft 27 tools and 6 pieces of armor. You place all of these items in 3 different chests for safe keeping. If you have an equal amount of items in all 3 chests, how many items are stored in each chest?

PVP SHOWDOWN

Which player earned the most experience points today? Solve the equations in each column then add up the answers to determine the winner of this PVP showdown.

1. $12 \div 6 =$ $16 \div 8 =$

2. $15 \div 3 =$ $9 \div 3 =$

3. $12 \div 4 =$ $18 \div 2 =$

4. $20 \div 5 =$ $14 \div 7 =$

5. $49 \div 7 =$ $42 \div 6 =$

6. $16 \div 4 =$ $18 \div 3 =$

TOTAL POINTS _____   _____

Circle the winner:

 ALEX    STEVE

DIVISION WITH 1- AND 2-DIGIT NUMBERS

(continued)

1. You need 12 Eyes of Ender to activate an End portal. You get 4 Eyes of Ender from every villager you trade with. How many villagers do you need to trade with to have enough Eyes of Ender to activate the End portal?

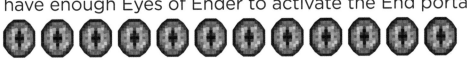

2. If each bowl of mushroom stew restores 2 hunger points, how many bowls do you need to eat to restore 24 hunger points?

3. If every snow golem drops 8 snowballs when destroyed, how many snow golems must be destroyed to get 64 snowballs?

4. If you can craft 9 boats a week using your resources, how many weeks will it take to craft 27 boats?

5.  There are 63 apples in your inventory today. Each horse on your farm needs to be fed 7 apples. How many horses can you feed?

6. To brew 4 potions of Water Breathing, you need 32 pufferfish. How many pufferfish do you need to make 1 potion of Water Breathing?

7. 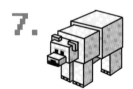 Every polar bear drops 6 fish when destroyed. If you need 36 fish, how many polar bears do you need to destroy?

8. You craft 5 jack-o-lanterns every day. If you have 35 jack-o-lanterns, how many days did you spend crafting them?

9.  Your farm has 42 cows. You divide them equally among 7 farms. How many cows do you keep on each farm?

10.  You encounter 54 creepers. You destroy 9 of them with each block of TNT you use. How many TNT blocks do you need to destroy all of the creepers?

11.  It takes you 81 minutes to craft 9 houses. How many minutes would you estimate it takes to craft each house?

12. Your cobblestone house has 20 windows. It has the same number of windows on all 4 walls of the house. How many windows does it have on each wall?

DIVISION WITH 1- AND 2-DIGIT NUMBERS

(continued from previous page)

13. Every time you enter the Nether fortress, you battle 3 wither skeletons. If you battle 36 wither skeletons, how many times did you enter the Nether fortress?

14. You place 8 rows of grass blocks. You use 32 grass blocks in all. How many grass blocks did you place in each row?

15. You use your enchantment table to enchant 56 swords and shovels. You enchant 7 items at a time. How many groups of items do you enchant?

HARDCORE MODE

A group of blazes in the Nether fortress shoots 54 fireballs at you. You dodge all of them. Another group of blazes shoot an additional 21 fireballs at you. You are hit by 12 of them. If each blaze can only shoot 3 fireballs, how many blazes did you battle?

PVP SHOWDOWN

Which player earned the most experience points today? Solve the equations in each column then add up the answers to determine the winner of this PVP showdown.

1. $81 \div 9 =$ $64 \div 8 =$

2. $30 \div 5 =$ $24 \div 4 =$

3. $92 \div 4 =$ $60 \div 5 =$

4. $36 \div 2 =$ $56 \div 8 =$

5. $40 \div 8 =$ $42 \div 6 =$

6. $21 \div 3 =$ $55 \div 11 =$

TOTAL POINTS _____   _____

Circle the winner:

 ALEX   STEVE

DIVISION WITH 1- AND 2-DIGIT NUMBERS

(continued from previous page)
Read the problem carefully. Use the pictures for extra help.
Write the answer in the space provided.

1.  You start a game with 34 hunger points. Every time you build a shelter, you lose 2 hunger points. How many shelters can you build before you lose all of your hunger points?

2.  You swing your sword 68 times, but it takes 17 swings to destroy each zombie. How many zombies can you destroy?

3.  Your wolves destroy a total of 64 creepers in the Overworld. If each of your wolves destroyed 4 creepers, how many wolves do you have?

4.  Squids drop 72 ink sacs into the water. You dive down to collect them, but you have to come up for air every time you collect 8 ink sacs. How many times do you come up for air as you collect all of the ink sacs?

5. You have 85 minutes until nightfall. It takes you 5 minutes to build a shelter. How many shelters can you build before nightfall?

6. You have 49 empty buckets. You put them into groups of 7 to fill with milk. How many groups of buckets do you have?

7. There are 90 ocelots in the Jungle Biome. A group of 5 ocelots is enough to scare away 1 creeper. How many creepers can all of the ocelots scare away?

8.

You want to craft 2 equally sized beacons using 56 blocks. How many blocks will you use for each beacon?

DIVIDING 1- AND 2-DIGIT NUMBERS

(continued from previous page)

9. You use 95 arrows to destroy a group of cave spiders. If it takes 5 arrows to destroy 1 cave spider, how many cave spiders were there in the group?

10. A group of creepers drops 44 units of gunpowder. Each creeper drops 2 units of gunpowder. How many creepers are in the group?

11. You find 76 cobwebs in an abandoned mineshaft. With each snip of your shears, you collect 4 cobwebs. How many snips does it take to collect all of the cobwebs?

12. A group of zombie pigmen drops 63 pieces of rotten flesh. If each zombie pigman drops 3 pieces of rotten flesh, how many zombie pigman are in the group?

13. A ghast hurls 81 fireballs at you and hits you every time. You die and respawn after being hit by 9 of them. How many times do you die and respawn?

14. You have 75 spawn eggs in your inventory. You use 15 of them every time you play. How many times do you play before running out of spawn eggs?

15. You are trying to build a 54-step staircase out of sandstone blocks. You stop after every 9 blocks to rest and eat something. How many times do you stop?

HARDCORE MODE
If each of a wither's 3 heads spit 18 skulls at you during a battle and you take damage every time 6 skulls are spit at you, how many times do you take damage?

PVP SHOWDOWN

Which player earned the most experience points today? Solve the equations in each column then add up the answers to determine the winner of this PVP showdown.

1.	$96 \div 6 =$	$76 \div 2 =$
2.	$45 \div 5 =$	$44 \div 11 =$
3.	$68 \div 4 =$	$16 \div 2 =$
4.	$9 \div 1 =$	$33 \div 3 =$
5.	$14 \div 7 =$	$81 \div 9 =$
6.	$64 \div 2 =$	$21 \div 7 =$
TOTAL POINTS	_____	_____

Circle the winner:

 ALEX    STEVE

MULTIPLYING AND DIVIDING WITHIN 100

Read the problem carefully. Use the pictures for extra help. Write the answer in the space provided.

1. You ride the minecart rail 2 times a day for 34 days. How many times do you ride the minecart rail?

2. You want to transport 36 chests to your base, but you can only transport 4 chests at a time. How many times do you need to transport groups of chests?

3.  You visit the Desert Biome 12 times more often than the Jungle Biome. If you visit the Jungle Biome 3 times, how many times do you visit the Desert Biome?

4. You have 49 splash potions. You need 7 splash potions to cure each zombie villager. How many zombie villagers can you cure?

MULTIPLYING AND DIVIDING WITHIN 100

(continued from previous page)

5. You use your new saddle to ride 7 groups of 6 pigs. How many pigs do you ride in all?

6. You collect 76 pieces of raw beef after destroying a group of mooshrooms. If each mooshroom drops 4 pieces of raw beef, how many mooshrooms did you destroy?

7. You drink 4 potions of Swiftness and 8 times as many potions of Strength. How many potions of Strength did you drink?

8. You visit the End 55 times. Every 5 times you visit, you find Elytra! How many times do you find Elytra?

9.  An iron golem drops 35 red flowers. A group of 7 villagers divides the flowers equally between themselves. How many flowers does each villager get?

10. 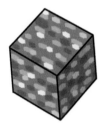 You want to mine 60 layers of diamond ore. If your pickaxe breaks after every 12 layers, how many times does your pickaxe break?

11.  You place 12 rows of 7 lapis lazuli ore blocks. How many lapis lazuli ore blocks do you place in all?

12. 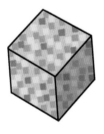 You place 30 iron blocks in 6 equal rows. How many iron blocks are in each row?

MULTIPLYING AND DIVIDING WITHIN 100

(continued from previous page)

13. You gather 21 ingredients to make a potion. You need 3 ingredients to make each bottle of potion. How many bottles of potion can you make?

14. You chop down a total of 63 trees. You build 7 beds from all of the wood. How many trees make a bed?

15. You destroy 10 mobs in one day in Survival mode. You destroy 8 times as many mobs the next day. How many mobs do you destroy the next day?

HARDCORE MODE

You want to make 23 cakes. Each one requires 3 milk and 2 sugar. You have 64 milk and 40 sugar. How much more do you need of each ingredient?

PVP SHOWDOWN

Which player earned the most experience points today? Solve the equations in each column then add up the answers to determine the winner of this PVP showdown.

1.	$27 \div 3 =$	$8 \times 1 =$
2.	$45 \div 5 =$	$4 \times 3 =$
3.	$8 \times 5 =$	$6 \div 2 =$
4.	$14 \div 2 =$	$21 \div 3 =$
5.	$34 \div 17 =$	$3 \times 9 =$
6.	$6 \times 4 =$	$42 \div 6 =$

TOTAL POINTS _____ _____

Circle the winner:

 ALEX   STEVE

MIXED OPERATIONS

Read the problem carefully. Write the answer in the space provided.

1. You craft 2 brewing stands, 5 beds, and 4 firework rockets each day for 2 days. How many items do you create in all?

2.  Over 4 days, you destroy 6 hostile mobs and 2 neutral mobs. If you destroy the same number of mobs each day, how many mobs do you destroy each day?

3. You have 4 diamonds in each of 8 chests. You collect 10 more diamonds while mining. How many diamonds do you have in all?

4.  You have 2 different farms. Each farm has 8 cows, 3 chickens and 7 horses. How many farm animals do you have in all?

5. There are 7 groups of 4 zombies approaching you. You destroy 16 zombies. How many zombies are left?

6.  You offer 9 emeralds to the first 3 villagers you meet and 6 emeralds to the next 4 villagers. How many emeralds do you offer for trade?

7. You build 8 beacons every day for 3 days. You build 12 beacons the next day. How many beacons do you build in all?

8.  You place 8 minecart rails in the morning and 5 times that amount in the afternoon. Creepers blow up half of the rails. How many rails are left?

MIXED OPERATIONS

(continued from previous page)

9. You battle 8 skeletons and 4 zombies one day and 2 groups of 3 creepers the next day. How many mobs do you battle in all?

10. You enchant 13 books and 4 swords every day for 2 days. You break 2 of the swords. How many enchanted items do you still have?

11. You shoot 7 arrows at a creeper and twice as many arrows at a giant zombie. Only 7 of them hit their target. How many arrows do not hit their target?

12. You see 6 groups of 5 creepers approaching. Before they get near you, 4 creepers explode. How many creepers are left?

13. Two witches each throw 3 potions of Slowness, 9 potions of Weakness, and 2 potions of Poison. How many potions are thrown in all?

14. You tame 7 groups of 5 ocelots and 3 groups of 6 horses. How many animals do you tame in all?

15. The Ender Dragon fires 4 Ender charges at you every time you enter the End. You enter the End 16 times one day and 5 times the next. How many Ender charges does the Ender Dragon fire in all?

HARDCORE MODE

You battle 16 ghasts and destroy half of them. The ones you destroy drop a variety of items. Half of them drop 2 gunpowder and the other half drop one ghast tear. How many items are dropped in all?

PVP SHOWDOWN

Which player earned the most experience points today? Solve the equations in each column then add up the answers to determine the winner of this PVP showdown.

1.	18 ÷ 9 =	6 + 8 =
2.	7 - 5 =	4 x 4 =
3.	9 + 4 =	6 ÷ 2 =
4.	5 x 1 =	3 - 3 =
5.	8 x 7 =	9 + 6 =
6.	16 ÷ 4 =	3 x 8 =

TOTAL POINTS _____   _____

Circle the winner:

 ALEX    STEVE

DIVISION WITH REMAINDERS

Read the problem carefully. Use the pictures for extra help. Write the answer in the space provided.

1. You have 43 experience points. You need 4 experience points to enchant a bow and arrow. How many bow and arrows can you enchant, and how many experience points will you have left over?

2.  You have 27 lily pads. You need 4 lily pads to help you cross each river. How many rivers can you cross with your lily pads and how many will be left over?

3. You plant 18 cactus blocks on your farm in rows of 5. How many rows do you plant, and how many blocks are left over?

4. You place 35 items in equal amounts in 4 different chests. How many items are in each chest and how many are left over?

DIVISION WITH REMAINDERS

(continued from previous page)

5. You trade with 7 different villagers in 44 minutes. If it takes the same amount of time to trade with each villager, how much time do you spend trading with each villager? How much time is left over after you've traded with all of them?

6.  You have 67 snowballs and want to make as many snow golems as you can. You need 8 snowballs to make every snow golem. How many snow golems can you make, and how many snowballs will you have left over?

7. It takes 6 swings of your axe to chop down every spruce tree. If you only have enough durability to swing your axe 58 times, how many trees can you chop down, and how many swings could you still take?

8. You collect 87 Ender pearls after battling a group of Endermen. You need 4 Ender pearls to make one Eye of Ender. How many Eyes of Ender can you make, and how many Ender pearls will be left over?

MULTIPLICATION AND DIVISION OF 2- AND 3-DIGIT NUMBERS

Read the problem carefully. Use the pictures for extra help. Write the answer in the space provided.

1.  You have 27 coal blocks to use in your furnace. If each block of coal can smelt 80 items, how many items can you smelt?

2.  You have 150 zombie eggs in your inventory. You use 15 of those eggs every day to spawn zombies. How many days pass before you run out of zombie eggs?

3. 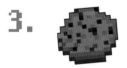 You lose 18 hunger points from exhaustion every day over 23 days of mining. How many hunger points do you lose over all 23 days?

4.  You brew 217 potions of Weakness. You need 7 potions to heal every zombie villager you meet. How many zombie villagers can you heal?

MULTIPLICATION AND DIVISION OF 2- AND 3-DIGIT NUMBERS

(continued from previous page)

5. You get 230 experience points from battling 5 skeletons. How many experience points do you estimate you get for battling each skeleton?

6. You have 196 wood planks. You need 7 wood planks to craft a boat. How many boats can you craft from all of your wood planks?

7. There are 122 donkeys total in the Plains Biome. If you bred them and tripled the number of donkeys in the Plains Biome, how many donkeys would there be?

HARDCORE MODE

Your dad says you can have 35 minutes of gaming time on every school day and 45 minutes of gaming time on each weekend day. Your mom says you can have 25 minutes of gaming time on every school day and 60 minutes on each weekend day. Which parent is offering you the most gaming time per week?

PVP SHOWDOWN

Which player earned the most experience points today? Solve the equations in each column then add up the answers to determine the winner of this PVP showdown.

1.	425 ÷ 5 =	126 ÷ 6 =
2.	315 ÷ 5 =	44 ÷ 4 =
3.	28 x 2 =	62 ÷ 2 =
4.	8 x 2 =	42 ÷ 6 =
5.	14 ÷ 7 =	19 ÷ 1 =
6.	16 x 6 =	3 x 44 =
TOTAL POINTS	_____	_____

Circle the winner:

 ALEX   STEVE

ADDING AND SUBTRACTING FRACTIONS

Solve the equations and simplify your answers.

1. You are attacked by a group of Endermen. You destroy $\frac{1}{4}$ of them with your sword and $\frac{2}{4}$ of them with your bow and arrow. What fraction of the Endermen did you destroy?

2. You battle a group of ghasts in the Nether. While you're battling, $\frac{1}{6}$ of their fireballs miss you and $\frac{4}{6}$ of them are deflected by your shield. The rest inflict damage. What fraction of fireballs inflict damage?

3.  You build $\frac{4}{8}$ of your cobblestone structure one day and $\frac{2}{8}$ of it the next day. What fraction of your cobblestone structure have you built in all?

4.  You use golden apples to cure $\frac{1}{16}$ of a group of zombie villagers. You craft a few more golden apples and cure another $\frac{4}{16}$ of the zombie villagers. What fraction of villagers have not been cured?

5. An iron golem destroys $\frac{1}{12}$ of a group of zombies. You destroy $\frac{3}{12}$ of the zombies. What fraction of the zombies are destroyed?

6. You use $\frac{3}{9}$ of your weapons in battle and $\frac{1}{9}$ of your weapons to mine valuable resources. What fraction of your weapons are still unused?

7.  You use your brewing stand to brew a bunch of potions. You use $\frac{1}{5}$ of the potions on blazes, $\frac{1}{5}$ on wither skeletons, and $\frac{1}{5}$ on zombie pigmen. What fraction of your potions do you use?

8. You enchant your armor for added protection. You enchant $\frac{3}{7}$ of your armor the first day and $\frac{3}{7}$ of your armor the next day. What fraction of your armor is not enchanted?

ADDING AND SUBTRACTING FRACTIONS WITH DIFFERENT DENOMINATORS

Make the fractions equivalent. Then add them or subtract them. Simplify your answers.

1. You battle a group of hostile mobs. If ⅙ of the hostile mobs fall in a lava pit and ³/₁₂ are destroyed by your arrows, what fraction of hostile mobs remain?

2. You use ⅑ of your gold ingots to make a clock and ⅔ of your gold ingots to make weapons. What fraction of your gold ingots do you use in all?

3. You use ¼ of your wooden sticks to make garden hoes. You use ⅓ of your wooden sticks to make arrows. What fraction of your wooden sticks remains?

4.  You battle the Wither often, but you lose ³/₅ of the times and run away ²/₆ of the times. The rest of the times, you win. What fraction of your battles do you win?

366

5.  You used ⁴/₇ of your diamonds to make armor and ¹/₃ of them to make weapons. What fraction of your diamonds did you use in all?

6. Your inventory is getting full. You know that ¹/₅ of your inventory is food, ¹/₄ of it is tools, and ¹/₂₀ of it is building materials. What fraction of your inventory is none of these things?

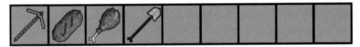

7. If you eat ⁴/₁₀ of your fish and use ²/₅ of your fish to tame ocelots, what fraction of your fish do you use in all?

HARDCORE MODE

Write your own word problem with fractions below and show it to your friend, your teacher, or your parent. Challenge him or her to solve it!

_____

_____

_____

_____

PVP SHOWDOWN

Which player earned the most experience points today?
Solve the equations in each column then add up the
answers to determine the winner of this PVP showdown.

1. $^1/_8 + ^2/_8 =$ $^1/_6 + ^2/_6 =$

2. $^1/_4 + ^1/_4 =$ $^3/_6 + ^2/_6 =$

3. $^3/_8 + ^4/_8 =$ $^2/_6 + ^2/_6 =$

4. $^3/_8 + ^1/_8 =$ $^1/_3 + ^1/_3 =$

5. $^4/_4 + ^6/_4 =$ $^9/_6 + ^8/_6 =$

TOTAL POINTS   _____   _____

Circle the winner:

 **ALEX**    **STEVE**

MULTIPLYING FRACTIONS BY A WHOLE NUMBER

Multiply and write the answer. Fractions should be written in their simplest form.

1. You battle 3 times against an army of husks using ¹/₆ of your weapons each time you battle. What fraction of your weapons do you use over the course of the battles?

2. You build 7 towers. Each time you build a tower, you use 1/8 of your gold ore. ¹/₈ gold ore. What fraction of your gold ore do you use in all?

3. You destroy ²/₃ the amount of spiders that your friend destroys. If your friend destroys 15 spiders, how many do you destroy?

4. Today you catch ²/₃ the amount of pufferfish that you caught yesterday. If you caught 6 pufferfish yesterday, how many do you catch today?

MULTIPLYING FRACTIONS BY A WHOLE NUMBER

(continued from previous page)

5.  You are attacked by 20 slimes one night and $^3/_{10}$ the amount of slimes the next night. How many slimes attacked you the second time?

6. 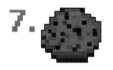 You and your tamed wolf battle a group of 15 endermites. Your wolf destroys $^1/_5$ of them and leaves the rest for you to battle. How many endermites do you battle?

7. You eat a bunch of cookies and gain $^1/_8$ of your 16 hunger points back. How many hunger points do you gain?

8.  In the course of a day, $^1/_6$ of the 48 witches you battle drop spider eyes. How many witches drop spider eyes?

9. You craft $\frac{2}{5}$ of your 75 houses with lapis lazuli ore. How many houses are made of lapis lazuli ore?

10. You spawn 54 creepers on your mob farm your first day of gaming and $\frac{1}{3}$ the amount of creepers the second day. How many creepers do you spawn the second day?

11. You destroy a group of chickens and collect 72 feathers. You use $\frac{1}{12}$ of the feathers to make arrows. How many feathers do you use?

12. You come across 42 spider webs and snip $\frac{1}{7}$ of them down with your shears. How many webs do you snip?

MULTIPLYING FRACTIONS BY A WHOLE NUMBER

(continued from previous page)

13. You see 74 animals in the Ice Plains Biome. You determine that ½ of them are polar bears. How many of them are polar bears?

14. You grow 81 flowers on your farm and ⅑ that amount of flowers in a field. How many flowers do you grow in a field?

15. You travel a distance of 40 blocks. You are wearing your Elytra wings for ⅕ of that journey. How many blocks do you travel wearing Elytra?

HARDCORE MODE

You eat 2½ cakes each day for 5 mornings to restore hunger points before a big day of mining. Over the next 4 days, you eat ½ of a cake each morning. How much cake do you eat over these 9 days?

PVP SHOWDOWN

Which player earned the most experience points today?
Solve the equations in each column then add up the
answers to determine the winner of this PVP showdown.

1. $\frac{1}{3} \times 6 =$ $8 \times \frac{2}{4} =$

2. $\frac{3}{5} \times 5 =$ $\frac{2}{3} \times 9 =$

3. $\frac{3}{4} \times 4 =$ $5 \times \frac{1}{5} =$

4. $\frac{1}{10} \times 5 =$ $3 \times \frac{2}{3} =$

5. $21 \times \frac{1}{7} =$ $\frac{2}{6} \times 6 =$

6. $8 \times \frac{1}{2} =$ $7 \times \frac{1}{7} =$

TOTAL POINTS _____   _____

Circle the winner:

 ALEX   STEVE

SOLVING FOR AREA

Use the equation provided to determine the area.

Area = length x width

1. Your farm is 8 feet long and 4 feet wide. What is the area of your farm?

2. You plant saplings on a section of grass that is 6 feet long and 5 feet wide. What is the area of your sapling farm?

3. The village library is 6 feet wide and 4 feet long. What is the area of the village library?

4. You discover a layer of redstone ore that is 8 feet long and 4 feet wide. What is the area of the layer?

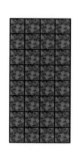

5. A skeleton patrols an area of the Nether fortress that is 9 feet long and 9 feet wide. What is the area of this section of the Nether fortress?

6. A pig will turn into a zombie pigman if lightning strikes anywhere inside his 4-foot-long, 4-foot-wide fenced area. What is the area inside the fence?

7. You mine a section of obsidian that is 4 feet long and 9 feet wide. What is the area of the obsidian?

8. A zombie falls in a pit that is 7 feet long by 6 feet wide. What is the area of the lava pit?

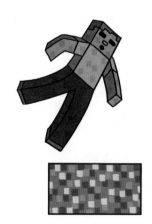

SOLVING FOR PERIMETER

You can find the perimeter of a 2-dimensional shape by adding all of its sides. Use the equations on the signs to help you solve these word problems.

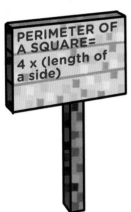

PERIMETER OF A SQUARE=
4 x (length of a side)

PERIMETER OF A RECTANGLE=
(2 x length) + (2 x width)

9. A creeper explodes and leaves a square opening in the ground that is 4 feet long. What is the perimeter of the opening?

10.  A zombie walks the edges of a rectangular shelter, trying to find an entrance. The shelter is 5 feet long and 7 feet wide. What is the perimeter of the shelter?

11.  You water a melon farm that is 8 feet long and 13 feet wide. What is the perimeter of the melon farm?

HARDCORE MODE

You know that the perimeter of a square desert temple room is 36 feet. You walk into another desert temple room with a perimeter that is double the length of the first room. How long is each wall in room 1? How long is each wall in room 2?

PVP SHOWDOWN

Which player's shelter has the greatest area? Solve the equations in each column to find the area of each room of their shelters and then add up the area of each room to determine the winner of this PVP showdown.

1. 7 ft. x 9 ft. =   7 ft. x 8 ft. =

2. 5 ft. x 5 ft. =   4 ft. x 6 ft. =

3. 3 ft.x 4 ft. =   5 ft. x 2 ft. =

4. 7 ft. x 2 ft. =   3 ft. x 3 ft. =

5. 5 ft. x 7 ft. =   9 ft. x 7 ft. =

6. 3 ft. x 6 ft. =   2 ft. x 8 ft. =

TOTAL SQUARE FOOTAGE _____   _____

Circle the winner:

 ALEX    STEVE

SOLVING FOR AREA AND PERIMETER

Use the formulas you've learned to solve for area or perimeter.

1. 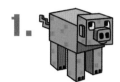 You keep your pigs in a pen that is 12 feet long and 5 feet wide. What is the area of the pig pen?

2.  You surround a valuable chest with a square border of TNT. Your TNT border is 15 feet long. What is the perimeter of your TNT border?

3.  You are trying to stay alive during a battle with a ghast. The danger zone where a ghast's fireballs can reach you is shaped like a rectangle. It's 17 feet long and 6 feet wide. What is the area of this danger zone?

4. 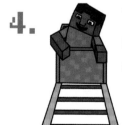 You want to build a rail system along the edges of a rectangular field that is 13 feet long and 10 feet wide. How many feet of rails do you need?

5. The square foundation of your cobblestone and wood house is 81 square feet. What is the length of one side of the foundation?

6. You want to avoid getting hit by a witch's splash potions. The rectangular splash zone is 8 feet long and 20 feet wide. What is the area of the witch's splash zone?

7. You harvest wheat on a farm that is 13 feet long and 7 feet wide. What is the area of your wheat farm?

8. A square end portal is 6 feet on every side. What is the perimeter of the end portal?

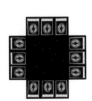

PVP ULTIMATE SHOWDOWN

Here is your final math challenge:
Go back and look at your calculations to see which avatar (Steve or Alex) won the most PVP battles. Circle the winner below.

With the help of your winning avatar and all of the experience points you've earned by practicing word problems, you've conquered the two boss mobs below.

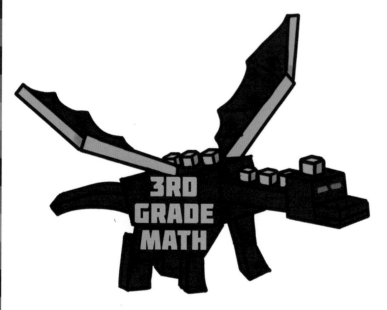

3RD GRADE MATH

4TH GRADE MATH

CONGRATULATIONS AND HAPPY MATH ADVENTURES!

ANSWER KEY

PAGE 324
1. 56 arrows
2. 24 silverfish
3. 16 fireballs
4. 30 unit of gunpowder

PAGE 325
5. 28 damage
6. 9 torches
7. 16 hearts
8. 27 swords

PAGE 326
9. 42 spiders
10. 15 pieces of rotten flesh
11. 16 gold ingots
12. 21 chests

PAGE 327
13. 30 obsidian blocks
14. 20 redstone ore blocks
15. 32 arrows
Hardcore mode
72 emeralds

PAGE 328
PVP Showdown
Alex: 162 experience points
Steve: 183 experience points

PAGE 329
1. 80 blocks
2. 45 times
3. 42 emeralds
4. 32 wolves

PAGE 330
5. 68 sheep
6. 44 experience points
7. 128 blocks
8. 75 Endermen

PAGE 331
9. 182 splash potions
10. 64 Endermen
11. 160 ocelots
12. 176 times

PAGE 332
13. 57 lapis lazuli
14. 45 ghasts
15. 203 arrows
Hardcore mode
126 active traps

PAGE 333
PVP Showdown
Alex: 411 experience points
Steve: 463 experience points

PAGE 334
1. 3 fish
2. 2 bats
3. 2 houses
4. 4 chests

PAGE 335
5. 3 eggs
6. 4 blocks
7. 3 villagers
8. 4 blocks

PAGE 336
9. 4 kinds
10. 6 Ender eye pearls
11. 8 times
12. 4 zombies

PAGE 337
13. 10 wolves
14. 8 minutes
15. 10 zombies
Hardcore mode
11 items

PAGE 338

PVP Showdown

Alex: 25 experience points

Steve: 29 experience points

PAGE 339

1. 3 villagers
2. 12 bowls
3. 8 snow golems
4. 3 weeks

PAGE 340

5. 9 horses
6. 8 pufferfish
7. 6 polar bears
8. 7 days

PAGE 341

9. 6 cows
10. 6 blocks
11. 9 minutes
12. 5 windows

PAGE 342

13. 12 times
14. 4 grass blocks
15. 8 groups of items

Hardcore mode

25 blazes

PAGE 343

PVP Showdown

Alex: 68 experience points

Steve: 45 experience points

PAGE 344

1. 17 shelters
2. 4 zombies
3. 16 tamed wolves
4. 9 times

PAGE 345

5. 17 shelters
6. 7 groups
7. 18 creepers
8. 28 blocks

PAGE 346

9. 19 cave spiders
10. 22 creepers
11. 19 snips
12. 21 zombie pigmen

PAGE 347

13. 9 times
14. 5 times
15. 6 times

Hardcore mode

9 times

PAGE 348

PVP Showdown

Alex: 85

Steve: 73

PAGE 349

1. 68 times
2. 9 times
3. 36 times
4. 7 zombie villagers

PAGE 350

5. 42 pigs
6. 19 mooshrooms
7. 32 potions of Strength
8. 11 times

PAGE 351

9. 5 flowers
10. 5 times
11. 84 lapis lazuli ore
12. 5 iron blocks

PAGE 352

13. 7 bottles
14. 9 trees
15. 80 mobs

Hardcore mode

5 milk, 6 sugar

PAGE 353

PVP Showdown

Alex: 91 Steve: 64

PAGE 354

1. 22 items
2. 2 mobs
3. 42 diamonds
4. 36 farm animals

PAGE 355

5. 12 zombies
6. 51 emeralds
7. 36 beacons
8. 24 rails

PAGE 356

9. 18 mobs
10. 32 enchanted items
11. 14 arrows
12. 26 creepers

PAGE 357

13. 28 potions
14. 53 animals
15. 84 Ender charges

Hardcore mode

12 items

PAGE 358

PVP Showdown

Alex: 82 Steve: 72

PAGE 359

1. 10 bow and arrows, 3 left over
2. 6 rivers, 3 lily pads left over
3. 3 rows, 3 cactuses left over
4. 8 items, 3 items left over

PAGE 360

5. 6 minutes, 2 minutes left over
6. 8 snow golems, 3 snowballs left over
7. 9 trees, 4 swings
8. 21 Eye of Ender, 3 Ender pearls left over

PAGE 361

1. 2,160 items
2. 10 days
3. 414 hunger points
4. 31 zombie villagers

PAGE 362

5. 46 experience points.
6. 28 boats
7. 366 donkeys

Hardcore mode

Dad: 265 Mom: 245 minutes

PAGE 363

PVP Showdown

Alex: 318 Steve: 221

PAGE 364

1. $3/4$ of the Endermen
2. $1/6$ of the fireballs inflict damage
3. $3/4$ of the cobblestone structure
4. $11/16$ of the villagers

PAGE 365

5. $1/3$ of the zombies
6. $5/9$ of your weapons
7. $3/5$ of your potions
8. $1/7$ of your armor

PAGE 366

1. $7/12$ of the hostile mobs remain
2. $7/9$ of your gold ingots
3. $5/12$ of your wooden sticks
4. $1/15$ of your battles

PAGE 367

5. $19/21$ of your diamonds
6. $1/2$ of your inventory
7. $4/5$ of your fish

PAGE 368

PVP Showdown

Alex: $38/8 = 4\,3/4$ **Steve: $33/6 = 5\,1/2$**

Hardcore mode

Answer may vary

PAGE 369

1. $\frac{1}{2}$ of your weapons
2. $\frac{7}{8}$ of the towers are gold ore
3. 10 spiders
4. 4 pufferfish

PAGE 370

5. 6 slimes
6. 12 endermites
7. 2 hunger points
8. 8 witches

PAGE 371

9. 30 houses
10. 18 creepers
11. 6 feathers
12. 6 webs

PAGE 372

13. 37 are polar bears
14. 9 flowers
15. 8 blocks

Hardcore mode

$14\frac{1}{2}$ cakes

PAGE 373

PVP Showdown
Alex: 15 1/2   **Steve: 16**

PAGE 374

1. 32 square feet
2. 30 square feet
3. 24 square feet
4. 32 square feet

PAGE 375

5. 81 square feet
6. 16 square feet
7. 36 square feet
8. 42 square feet

PAGE 376

9. 16 feet
10. 24 feet
11. 42 feet

Hardcore mode

room 1: 9 feet long   room 2: 18 feet long

PAGE 377

PVP Showdown
Alex: 167 square feet   **Steve: 178 square feet**

PAGE 378

1. 60 square feet
2. 60 feet
3. 102 square feet
4. 46 feet

PAGE 379

5. 9 feet
6. 160 square feet
7. 91 square feet
8. 24 feet

PAGE 380

Steve (6 wins)   Alex (5 wins)